THE MISHINGS
(Miris)
OF ASSAM
Development of A New Lifestyle

THE MISHINGS (Miris) OF ASSAM

Development of A New Lifestyle

JATIN MIPUN

GYAN

Published by

GYAN

Gyan Publishing House
5, Ansari Road
Daryaganj, New Delhi-110002
Phone: 011-47034999, 9811692060
E-mail: books@gyanbooks.com

Distribution Network
gyanbooks.com
India, USA, Canada, UK, Australia, France

ISBN: 978-93-6280-660-4 (PB)

First Published, 2024

Printed at: Gyan Press, Delhi.

The Mishings (Miris) Of Assam: Development of a New Lifestyle
Author: Jatin Mipun

FOREWORD

Socio-cultural changes because of culture-contact through different media are inevitable in the modern dynamic world. Dynamism is a sign of progress. The individuals as well as groups are exposed to these changed situations and hence adjustments become necessary for survival. But the processes and factors involved are always not identical in all the situations. Therefore, it is interesting to know what is happening where and among whom. The author has looked at the Mishing life from this point of view. By studying three villages in detail he has attempted to project the changing situation in the tribe.

The Mishing is a major tribe of Assam, the homeland of a large number of populations, both tribal and non-tribal, of different ethnic origins, linguistic affiliations and having varied socio-cultural traditions since long past. There has always been socio-cultural as well as biological interaction among these populations, and as a result the tribes are at different levels of modernization. The influence of Hinduism is very strong among many tribes. Among these some members have accepted Hinduism, while others are Hinduised.

The neo-Vaisnavite movement was launched by the great Assamese saint Srimanta Sankardeva in the later part of the fifteenth century. Gradually it started gaining momentum and was spread to different parts of this region of the country. It had great impact on the Mishings as well. They accepted Neo-Vaisnavism, though side by side they followed some of their traditional rites and rituals. The neo-Vaisnavite faith brought remarkable changes in the socio-cultural life of the Mishing. The author has found this to be the strongest force for acculturation.

The Mishing have their own lauguage, but they have accepted the Assamese language to a great extent. Many of the neo-Visnavite literature are written in old Assamese, and hence learning of Assamese helped the Mishings of understand the new ideas, beliefs, practices, etc. Thus religion helped in the spread not only of Assamese language, but also the Hindu way of life among them.

It is a known fact that different types of communication network break the isolation and bring different populations closer. In this process several factors are associated. The author has clearly demonstrated how these factors are interacting to bring changes in the Mishing society.

The process of acculturation and improved communication system have accelerated the pace of development of the Mishing people. They are no longer an isolated community, but has become a part of the greater whole. The noteworthy changes in their attitude towards economy, education, health practices and the like have helped in the overall development of the Mishings under study. However, the author nhas observed that the present processes operating in the Mishing society have widened the distance between the rich and poor sections and have created new elites among the Mishings, a situation which deserves special consideration.

Dr Jatin Mipun deserves congratulations for his presenting such a vivid picture of the socio-cultural changes in the Mishing tribe and analysing the forces and factors involved in the process by undertaking an in-depth study. Such work among the tribes in this part of the country are rare. The book will be a valuable addition to the existing literature on the sociology and ethnography of north eastern India.

Department of Anthropology
Gauhati University

B M DAS

PREFACE

The study on socio-cultural change among the tribes of India is always fascinating. Numerous studies have been conducted on interaction and social change, highlighting the result of contact between the literate and preliterate, between the primitive and civilized and between tribes and non-tribes.

In Assam, the interaction between the non-tribal Assamese population and the Mishings have been taking place for the last several centuries. The Mishings were originally hill dwellers in Arunachal Pradesh. After their shift to the plains of Assam, they became the part of the regional Assamese culture. It has happened due to acculturation and the impact of growing communication. In this study, an attempt has been made to analyse the interrelationship between acculturation, communication and development with special reference to the Mishings.

In my research work, I received help from different sources. I am thankful to the University of Dibrugarh for providing me a research fellowship (1976-79) which greatly helped me in conducting my research work. I express my sincere gratefulness and indebtedness to my teacher and supervisor Dr. S.M. Dubey, M.A. Ph.D. Professor and Head of the Department of Sociology, Dibrugarh University, for his guidance and stimulating suggestions throughout the entire course of the study without which the work would have not been completed.

I am also grateful to Dr. D. Doley, Dr. C.K. Gogoi, other teachers and research scholars of the Department of Sociology who offered help, suggestions and encouragement from time to time. I joined government service in 1979 and while I was busy in official duty, Sri O.P. Agarwal I.A.S., Sri S. Thakur, A.C.S. and numerous other friends helped and encouraged me to complete this study. I am thankful to them.

I extend my thanks also to Sri T. Dihingia and Sri T. Bhuyan who helped me from time to time in typing out the chapters. I must express my thanks to Sri K. Gogoi for typing out the final draft of the chapters of this dissertation.

I shall be failing in my duty if I do not thank the villagers and respondents of this study who helped me from all sides. I shall continue to remember their love and affection.

Jatin Mipun

CONTENTS

	Foreword	*(v)*
	Preface	*(vii)*
1.	Introduction	1
2.	Mishings : A Portrait of the Traditional Social System	15
3.	The Field of Study and Methodology	32
4.	Social Background of the Respondents	44
5.	Acculturation Among the Mishings	54
6.	Impact of Modern Communication	77
7.	Socio-Economic Development	97
8.	Overview and Concluding Remarks	121

Appendices

I	Bibliography	129
II	Village Schedule	145
III	Glossary	159
	Index	

CHAPTER I

INTRODUCTION

I

The Mishings are an Indo-Mongoloid tribe settled in the plains of Assam. Originally, they were hill dwellers and lived along with the Adis in Arunachal Pradesh. On the basis of the legends of the tribe and available historical records, they moved to the plains of Assam, around the 13th century A.D. Still, they retain their mythological, linguistic and institutional affinity with the Adis and the Nisis of Arunachal Pradesh. After their migration to the plains, considerable changes have taken place in their ecology, pattern of adaptation, cultivation, language, rituals, dress and house construction. The residence in the plains has offered them a better system of communication. The present dissertation is an attempt in understanding the process of acculturation, communication and development among the Mishings of Assam.

In the social sciences, the concept of 'acculturation' gained currency during the late nineteenth century. For the first time, Powell (1880) wrote of the 'force of acculturation' which was about 'changing indigenous traditions under the influence of civilized people'. McGee (1898) discusses later on about 'piratical acculturation' by which he meant 'cultural interchange under advantageous condition.' In the writings of the earlier twentieth century, the term was often employed interchangeably with diffusion and assimilation. In the British studies, it was used in terms of 'culture contact'. Though various studies have already been conducted on culture contact and social change, only in the early part of the twentieth century, Redfield, Linton and Herskovitz (1936) attempted to draw for the first time a systematic definition of the concept. According to them—

> Acculturation includes those phenomena which result when groups of individuals having different cultures come into continuous first hand contact, with subsequent change in the original cultural patterns of either or both groups (1936:149).

In spite of much criticism, the definition formulated by them has been able to pave the way for the future study of acculturation in different societies. In the middle part of the twentieth century, Herskovitz (1955:472) stressed on acculturation as the 'study of culture transmission in process' and tried to assess the levels of material cultures of different societies. Murdock (1955:3) has defined the term as the 'assumption of culture through contact', especially with the people of higher civilization'. Spindler (1955:3-4) expands the definition of the term as

> the total adaptive process that occurs in cultural patterning and value system, group alignments, systems of control, social organization, and economy and in the psychological structures and functions of individuals, as adoptions are made to the changing conditions of existence created by the impact of populations and their cultures upon each other.

Having lots of criticisms and modifications of the definition of the term, social scientists have, however, accepted acculturation as an important aspect of the study of social change which especially denotes the transformation of cultural or social elements from one society to another (Beals: 1951; Eaton:1952; Keesing:1964; Hallowell:1957; McGee:1960; Gould and Kolb:1964; Moore:1965;Task and Nelson:1974; Lewis:1976; Friedle: 1976).

In the world perspectives, various works have been conducted on the process of acculturation in different societies (e.g. Mead: 1932; Herskovitz: 1938; Linton: 1940; Malinowski:1945; Sharp: 1952; Redfield: 1953; Newcomb: 1956; Bacon and Herskovitz: 1959; Wilson and Wilson; 1965; Alba: 1976). In this context, Mead's study of the plains Indians (1930) and Herskovitz's study of Carebeans (1938) are of special significance. As the plains Indians were not in the position to adjust with the demands of new culture, Mead tried to see the problems of disorganisation as a result of contact. She pointed out how the Indian indigenous religious practices suffered due to the settlements of whites with the Indians. Due to the acceptance of Presbyterianism, the American Indians were regarded neither as the followers of indigenous religion nor Presbyterianism. Amidst this situation, Mead discussed the disorganisation and disintegration of the traditional way of life which was the product of the culture contact between the whites and the Indians. Herskovitz's major concern was with the reinterpretation of the new cultural elements so that it can be adjusted with the traditional culture of the people. He pointed out that the blacks have always tried to find out relationship between their African Gods and the Catholic saints. The ultimate result is the acculturation among the blacks in spite of their obligations to old norms and values.

On the basis of the studies of Mead and Herskovitz on acculturation, the following conclusions have been derived:

(a) The acculturation results as a contact between two societies or cultures where the dominant culture often influences the weaker or primitive culture.

(b) As a result of the influence of the dominant culture, the weaker culture is either changed totally or gradually.

(c) The contact between the dominant and the weak cultures leads to disorganisation of the religious practices and the traditional way of life of the latter. It creates marginality among the members of the weak culture.

(d) In certain situations, the people belonging to the weak culture try to find out the common elements between their culture and the dominant culture.

The main focus of this study is to analyse the process and impact of contact between a tribe with features of primitive organisations (micro level), regional Assamese culture with distinct language, polity and productive system: middle range or regional) and the great tradition and high culture (the macro level, the Indian tradition and culture represented through Hinduism, mythology, beliefs, rituals and social organisation). For the analysis of the influence of Hinduism among the Mishings, various aspects such as religious practices and social institutions have been considered. Moreover, the influence of the regional Assamese culture on their housing pattern, food habit, dress, language and in tools and implements are also considered for the discussion of acculturation among the Mishings in Assam. The aim of including all these aspects is to see the total process of culture change among the Mishings. As they came in contact with the Hinduism through regional culture, the other dominant group tried to apply the notions of purity and pollution (the caste system). They picked up the beliefs and myths and social organisation of the great tradition of Hinduism.

II

The term communication refers to the materials, mechanical systems, media of mass-communication and interpersonal linkages used for the transmission of messages. It is difficult to give a definition for this concept.

Some social psychologists and sociologists have confined their interests in communication largely to the study of languages and the analysis of the vehicles and messages in communication, although they have also been interested in the functional effects of communication (Lundberg, Schrag and Larsen: 1954, 360; Quine: 1960; Newman: 1966,62).

In the field of communication, several works have been conducted by the social scientists (e.g. Ayer: 1955; Damle: 1955; Broadbent: 1958; Crowly: 1962; Dexter: 1964; Schramm: 1967; Dube: 1967; Mishra: 1973; Bhattacharyya: 1976; Atal: 1977; Hockings: 1977). In Indian situation, the works of Damle (1955), Dube (1967) and Bhattacharyya (1976) are significant. Damle conducted his study in the early fifties in six Indian villages. One of the major findings in his study is that the villages which had an idea and interest in communication, were more informative and alert. They were in a position to inform the author about the situation of Indian villages of that time. But the main problem, as raised by the author, is that the situation was not there whereby the villagers could know the significance of communication in their development.

The study of Dube: (1967b) on communication, innovation and planned change in India is also remarkable in this field. This study shows the relationship between innovation, planned change and media of communication. Bhattacharyya discusses how, with the introduction of satellite communication, people of the world have come into closer contact. According to him, the world organizations like U.N., UNESCO and others have been playing a cardinal role in the field of global communication.

The role of communication is extremely significant in acculturation and development.

For the purpose of the present study, the communication has been divided into the following two parts:

(a) the traditional communication which includes oral system of communications, transport (elephants, boats), messengers and announcement through drum beating etc., and

(b) the modern system of communication includes formal and written communication, post and telegram, transport (roads and rails), mass-media (radio, newspapers and cinema).

III

The term development is frequently used by the economists and other social scientists. But the theoretical framework of the term 'development' in sociological perspective has emerged only a few years back when the emphasis was laid on non-economic and human factors (Eisenstadt: 1961; Smelser: 1963; Barringer: 1965; Bhumer: 1966; Horowitz : 1966; Aron: 1967). It is to be noted that most of the contemporary social scientists have concentrated on the societal development (Gresinger: 1971; Havers: 1971; Warner: 1971; Elberts and Young: 1971) and the significant role of value in development (Von Wiese: 1956:, Horowitz ; 1966; Myrdal : 1968). Moreover, sociological theory on development has given emphasis on the 'Statios' to 'dynamics' of society (Moore: 1960a; Parsons: 1961; Martindale: 1962; Horowitz: 1966; Hobbs: 1971).

A few social scientists have regarded development as a type of social change (Greiger: 1971; Havens: 1971; Warner: 1971). Others have given emphasis on normative aspects (Seers : 1970; Warner : 1971; Kim : 1973). According to Seers (1971: 1-2):

> Development is inevitably treated as a normative concept, as almost synonym for improvement, to pretend otherwise is just to hide one's value judgments.

Kim (1973) discusses development by giving emphasis on the following aspects:

(a) development as value concept;

(b) development as societal structural change; and

(c) importance of political leadership in development process.

How the value perspectives have been helping in the change of personal values and thus help in attitudinal change are analysed by the social scientists from various angles (Weber: 1958; Lerner: 1958; Hoselitz: 1960; McClelland: 1961; Boulding: 1963; Warshay: 1964; Inkles: 1966; Kahl: 1968; Myrdal: 1968; Kim: 1973). However, it is agreed upon by the social scientists that the term 'development' is an ideal goal in itself.

One of the best examples in the field of value judgment and societal development is Max Weber's (1958) monumental work 'The Protestant Ethic and the Spirit of Capitalism'. The author discusses the relationship between Capitalism and Protestantism on the basis of historical evidence, and thereby he tries to analyse the effects of Protestantism in the growth of Capitalism. Weber shows that there is a closer relationship between religion and economic ethics. The basic issue as propagated by him is that something is there in Protestantism which helps create the system of economic norms, which lead to rationality and acquisitiveness. The other religions of the world lack this spirit according to Max Weber.

Another noteworthy work on development is Myrdal's 'Asian Drama' (1968). In his study Myrdal attempted to give an actual picture and prospects for developments in the South Asian countries. After the Second World War, numerous attempts have been made by Governments of South Asian countries for the development of their respective States. In his three volumes, Myrdal tries to include almost all the aspects responsible for the backwardness of the countries of South Asia.

For the purpose of the present study, the development includes :

1. The development in socio-cultural activities.
2. The development in occupation and the subsidiary occupation adopted by the respondents.
3. Agricultural innovation and alternatives for self-sufficiency and the learning of investment of income.
4. Acceptance of medical science and family planning.
5. Respondents' education and preference of education for their children.
6. The attitude of the respondents towards development.

IV

Since the early part of the twentieth century, various studies have been conducted dealing with social change among the Indian tribes. The sociologists and the anthropologists who first paved the way for empirical and systematic study of social change among the tribes in Indian situation were Chattopadhyaya (1922a), Majumder (1937), Karve (1942), Srinivas (1942a), Ghurye (1943b, 1952c). These studies did not use the term 'acculturation'. In place of it, they often used the term 'cultural change', 'social change', and so on. By studying the process of change among the Indian tribes, Ghurye (1963b) says that in spite of the expected changes among the tribes, they are the sufferer of stresses and strains resulting out of conversion to Hinduism. Srinivas (1966c) discusses the pattern of social change in India by using few terms and models, e.g., Sanskritization and Westernization. As indicated above, without using the term 'acculturation' Indian social scientists studied the problem of 'culture-contact' through the concepts of social and cultural change.

Several scholars (Ghurye: 1940a; Mehra: 1954; Dutta Majumder: 1956; Srinivas: 1961b; Jay: 1961; Sinha: 1962; Sahay: 1962 and others) have conducted researches to assess the impact of the contact between Hinduism and tribal communities in India. As commented by Vidyarthi,

> Three distinct processes have been usually studied and noted: (1) the renunciation of certain tribal practices and adoption of others followed by higher castes, (2) the creation of legends and myths of ancient Hindu tradition, and (3) the exercise of economic and political dominance wherever possible in seeking recognition to a higher status (1978 : 440).

Along with the former studies on culture contact, the studies on acculturation among the tribes of India have also been conducted with equal enthusiasm by several social scientists (Sachchidanand: 1964; Agarwal: 1968; Aurora: 1972; Vidyarthi and Rai: 1977).

Alike the field of acculturation, various studies have been conducted in Indian situation on the field of communication also. In this context, the studies of Damle (1955), Dube (1967b), Bhattacharyya (1976), Atal (1977), Hockings (1977) are worth mentioning. Of course, numerous studies on inter-tribal and tribal-non-tribal relationship have been conducted by various authors which depended mostly on the study of communication system. From this point of view the studies of Dasgupta: (1961), Furer Haimendorf (1962), Das (1967), Majumder (1972), Goswami (1972), Dubey (1972a) are noteworthy.

There are several studies on tribal development (Chattopadhyay : 1949; Dube : 1949a; Kulkarni : 1964; Aurora : 1972; Goswami: 1972; Vidyarthi and Rai: 1976; Dubey: 1976b). But so far as the plains tribes of Assam in general and the Mishings in particular are concerned, no systematic study has been conducted uptil now. Only a few books, monographs, papers (Robinson: 1841; Hunter: 1879; Michell: 1883; Waddell: 1901; Baines: 1912; Payengkataki: 1935; M'Cosh: 1937; Pegu: 1956; Doley: 1973; Bhandari: 1974; Sharma Thakur: 1976), census reports are found on the Mishings. In the monographs written by the early British administrators, there are preliminary reports about the Mishings. Payengkataki (1935) and Pegu (1956) have tried to depict the social and cultural picture of the Mishings. Really, a few studies have been conducted dealing with culture and development of the Mishings (Doley: 1973; Bhandari : 1974; Sharma Thakur : 1976; Pegu: 1981).

The major aim of the present study is to highlight the interrelationship between the three variables - acculturation, communication and development - in the contexts of Mishings, a tribe in Assam. It is an attempt to see how the two independent variables 'acculturation' and 'communication' have influenced the dependent variable 'development'.

Both the independent variables 'acculturation' and 'communication' are correlated with each other. Without communication, acculturation is impossible and the continuity of the process of acculturation means the presence of communication in between two societies with different cultures. The development cannot be a reality in a society without the former variables.

The author through the present study wants to fill up the gap of inadequacy by probing into the process of acculturation, communication and development among the Mishings.

References

Alba, Richard D.
1976 Social Assimilation among American Catholic National Origin Groups. American Sociological Review 6, Vol. 41.

Ayer, A.J. and others
1955 Studies in Communication. London: Secker & Warburg.

Aron, Raymond
1967 The Industrial Society. New York: Praeger.

Agrawal, B.C.
1968 From Commerce to Conquest : A Historical Study of Acculturation in India. The Eastern Anthropologist 1, Vol. XXI, Jan-April.

Aurora, G.S.
1977 Communication and Nation-building in India. In M.N. Srinivas and others (eds.), Dimensions of Social Change in India. Allied Publishers Pvt. Ltd., Bombay.

Beals, Ralph L.
1951 Urbanism, Urbanization and Acculturation. American Anthropologist, New Series 53:1-10

Bacon, W.R. and M.J. Herskovitz (eds.)
1959 Continuity and Change in African Cultures.

Broadbent, Donal E.
1958 Perception and Communication. New York : Pergamon.

Bhattacharyya, V.R.
1976 Communication in a Global Village. Chetana Publications, New Delhi.

Barringer, H.R., G.I. Blankston and R.W. Mark
1965 Social Change in Developing Areas. Cambridge, Massachusetts : Schenkman Publishing Company.

Bhumar, Herbert
1966 The Idea of Social Development. Studies in Comparative International Development 2:3-11.

Boulding, Kenneth, K.
1963 The Image Aun Arbor : University of Michigan Press.

Baines, Sir A.

1912 Ethnography (Castes and Tribes). Concept Publishing Co., Delhi.

Bhandari, J.S.

1974 Land and Social Structure : An Economic Study of a Mishing Village. In K.S. Mathur and B.C. Agrawal (eds.), Tribe, Caste and Peasantry. Ethnographic and Folk Culture Society, U.P., Lucknow.

Crowly, Thomas H.

1962 Modern Communication. New York : Columbia University Press.

Chattopadhyay, K.P.

1922a An Essay on the History of Newal Culture. Journal of Proceeding of Asiatic Society of Bengal (New series), Vol. XXIII, No. 3.

1949b The Tribal Problem and its Solution. The Eastern Anthropologist 1, Vol. III, September.

Damle, Y.B.

1955 Communication of Modern Ideas and Knowledge in Indian Villages. Deccan College, Poona.

Dexter, L.A. and David M. White (eds.)

1964 People, Society and Mass Communication. New York, Free Press.

Dube, S.C.

1949a Some Aspects of Tribal Problems. The Eastern Anthropologist 1, Vol. III, September.

1967b A Note on Communication, Innovation and Planned Change in India. In Daniel Lerner and W. Schramm (eds.), Communication and Change in the Developing Countries. East West Centre, Honolulu.

1977c Tribal Heritage of India (eds.). Vol. I: Ethnicity, Identitv and Interaction. Vikas Publishing House, Pvt. Ltd., New Delhi.

Dubey, S.M.

1972a Education, Social Change and Political Consciousness among the Tribes of North East India. In K.S. Singh (ed.), Tribal Situation in India. Indian Institute of Advanced Study, Simla.

1967b Modernization among the Tribes of North Eastern India (Assam). In S.K. Srivastava (ed.), Tradition and Modernization. Indian International Publications, Allahabad.

Dutta Majumder, N.

1956 The Santhal. Calcutta, Anthropological Survey of India.

Das, B.M.

1967 Assamese Culture and the Hill People of North East India. In R. Mitra and B. Das Gupta (eds.), A Common Perspective for North-East India. Calcutta: Pannalal Das Gupta.

Doley, D.

1973 The Socio-economic Life of the Miri Tribe. North Eastern Research Bulletin, Vol. IV, Summer.

Eston, Joseph W.

1952 Controlled Acculturation : A Survival Technique of the Hutterites. American Sociological Review 17:331-340.

Eisenstadt, S.N.

1961 Essays on the Sociological Aspects of Political and Economic Development. The Hague, Monton.

Eberts, P.R. and Frank, W. Young

1971 Sociological Variables of Development : Their Range and Characteristics. In G.M. Beal, R.C. Powers and E.W. Coward Jr. (eds.), Sociological Perspectives of Domestic Development. Ames : Iowa State University Press.

Friedle, John

1976 Cultural Anthropology. Harper's College Press, A Department of Harper and Row Publications, New York.

Furer-Haimendorf, Christoph von

1962 The Apatanis and their Neighbourhood. London : Routledge and Kegan Paul.

Gould J. and W.L. Kolb

1964 A Dictionary of Social Sciences. The Free Press.

Greiger, H. Kent

1971 Societal Development : Notes on the Vestment of a Concept. In G.M. Beal, R.C. Powers and E.W. Coward Jr. (eds.), Sociological Perspectives of Domestic Development. Ames: Iowa State University Press.

Ghurye, G.S.

1940a Caste and Class in India. Bombay: Popular Book Depot.

1945b The Aborigines - So Called and Their Future. Institute of Politics and Economics, Poona.

1952c Social Change in Maharashtra, Part-I, Sociological Bulletin 1, Vol. VI.

1963d The Scheduled Tribes. Popular Prakashan, Bombay.

Goswami, B.B.

1972 The Tribes of Assam : Few Comments on their Social and Cultural Ties with the Non-tribes. In K. Suresh Singh (ed.), Tribal Situation in India (Proceeding of a Seminar). Institute of Advance Study, Simla.

Herskovitz, M.J.

1938a Acculturation : The Study of Culture Contact. New York : J.J. Augustin.

1955b Cultural Anthropology (An Abridged Revision of Man and His Work). Oxford and I.B.H. Publishing Co., Delhi.

Hallowell, A.I.

1957 Socio-psychological Aspects of Acculturation. In R. Linton (ed.), The Science of Man in the World Crisis. New York: Columbia University Press.

Hockings, Paul

1977 Communication Networks. In M.N. Srinivas and others (ed.), Dimensions of Social Change in India. Allied Publishers Pvt. Ltd., Bombay.

Horowitz, I.L.

1966 Three Worlds of Development. In G.M. Beal, R.C. Powers and E.W. Coward Jr. (eds.), Sociological Perspectives of Domestic Development. Ames: Iowa State University Press.

Hobbs, D.J.
1971 Some Contemporary Sociological Perspectives Regarding Social Change. In ibid.

Hoselitz, B.P.
1960 Sociological Aspects of Economic Growth. New York: The Free Press of Glencoe.

Hunter, W.W.
1879 A Statistical Account of Assam. Vol. II, Trubner and Co., London. Reprinted 1975 by B.B. Publishing Corporation, Delhi.

Inkles, Alex
1966 Modernization of Man. In M. Weiner (ed.), Modernization. New York: Basic Books.

Jay, Edward
1961 Revitalization Movement in Tribal India. In L.P. Vidyarthi (ed.), Aspects of Religion in Indian Society. Meerut: Kedar Nath Ram Nath.

Keesing, F.M.
1954 Acculturation : An Exploratory Formulation. American Anthropologist, Vol. 54.

Kim, Kyong Dong
1975 Towards a Sociological Theory of Development : A Structural Perspective. Rural Sociology 4, Vol. 38, Winter.

Kahl, Joseph A.
1968 The Measurement of Modernization. Austin : University of Texas Press.

Kulkarni, M.G.
1974 Problems of Tribal Development : A Case Study. Parimal Prakashan, Aurangabad.

Karve, Irawati
1942 Some Studies in the Making of Culture Patterns. In J.R. Mills and others (eds.), Essays in Anthropology, presented to Rai Bahadur S.C. Roy. Lucknow: Maxwell & Co.

Lewis, Russell E.
1976 Controlled Acculturation Revisited : An Examination of Differential Acculturation and Assimilation between the Hutterian Brethren and the Old Order Amish. In International Review of Modern Sociology 1, Vol. 6, Spring.

Lundberg, G.A., C.C. Schrag and O.N. Lersen
1954 Sociology. New York: Harper and Brothers.

Linton, Ralph
1940 Acculturation in Seven American India Tribes.

Lerner, Daniel
1958 The Passing of Traditional Society. New York: Free Press.

Moore, W.E.
1960a A Reconsideration of Theory of Social Change. American Sociological Review 6, Vol. 25, December.
1965b Social Change. Prentice Hall of India (Pvt.) Ltd., New Delhi.

McGee, W.J.

1960 Piratical Acculturation. In American Anthropologist, Selected Papers from the American Anthropologist, 1888-1920. Evanston III : Row, Peterson. (First published in Vol. II of the American Anthropologist, New Series.

Mead, Margaret

1932 The Changing Culture of an Indian Tribe. New York : Columbia University Press.

Majumder, D.N.

1937 A Tribe in Transition : A Study in Culture Patterns. London: Logman Green & Co.

Mishra, V.M.

1973 The Communication Media and Learning for Modernization : A Conceptual Model, p.128 in Indian Journal of Social Research 2, Vol. XIV, August.

Myrdal, G.

1968 Asian Drama. Penguin Books, U.K.

Martindale, Don

1962 Social Change and Cultural Change. Princeton, New Jersey : D. Van Nostrand.

McClelland, David C.

1961 The Achieving Society. Princeton, New Jersey : D. Van Nastrand.

Mehra, J.D.

1954 The Naiks of Ramgarh and the Effects of Acculturation on them. p. 33 in the Anthropologist 1, Vol. I, August.

Majumder, D.N.

1972 A Study of Tribe/Caste Continuum and the Process of Sanskritization among the Bodo-Speaking Tribes of the Garo Hills. In K.S. Singh (ed.), Tribal Situation in India. Institute of Advance Study, Simla.

Murdock, G.P.

1955 On the Definition of Acculturation. In H.P. Fairchild (ed.), Dictionary of Sociology. Ames. Iowa : Littlefield, Adms.

Malinowski, Bronislow

1945 The Dynamics of Culture Change : An Enquiry into the Race Relations in Africa. New Haven: Yale University Press.

Michell, John F.

1883 The North East Frontier of India (A Topographical, Political and Military Report). Reprinted 1973 by Vivek Publishing House, Delhi.

M'Cosh, John

1957 Topography of Assam. Reprinted 1975 by Sanskaran Prakashak, Delhi.

Newcomb, W.W.

1956 The Culture and Acculturation of the Dalware Indians.

Newman, John B.

1966 A Rationale for a Definition of Communication. In Alfred G. Smith (ed.), Communication and Culture. Holt, Rinehart and Winston, New York.

Parsons, Talcott

1961 Some Considerations on the Theory of Social Change. Rural Sociology 26, September.

Pavegkataki, S.

1955 *Miri Jatir Buranji* (History of the Miris). Momoi Bebejia, Dhemaji.

Pegu, N.C.

1956 The Miris or the Mishings of the Brahmaputra Valley. Kumarbari, Majuli, Assam.

1981 The Mishings of the Brahmaputra Valley, Dibrugarh, Assam.

Powell, J.W.

1880 Introduction to the Study of Indian Languages. Washington D.C., Government Printing Office.

Quine, Willard Van Orman

1960 Ward and Object. Cambridge, Mass: The MIT Press, New York : Wiley.

Redfield, R., R. Linton, M.J. Herskovitz

1936 Memorandum on the Study of Acculturation. American Anthropologist 38, pp.149-52.

Robinson, W.

1841 A Descriptive Account of Assam. Reprinted 1975 by Sanskaran Prakashak, Delhi.

Redfield, Robert

1955 The Primitive World and its Transformation. Ithaca, New York: Cornell University Press.

Sharp, Lauriston

1952 Steel Axes for Stone-Age Australians. Human Organization 11:17-22.

Smelser, Neil J.

1963 Mechanism of Change and Adjustment to Change. In B.E. Hoselitz and W.E. Moore (eds.), Industrialisation and Society. Paris--the Hague; UNESCO, Monton.

Seers, D.

1970 The Meaning of Development. The Agricultural Development Council Reprint (September).

Srinivas, M.N.

1942a Marriage and Family in Mysore. Bombay.

1961b Dominant Caste in Rampura. American Anthropologist 1, Vol. 61.

1966c Social Change in Modern India. Berkeley and Los Angeles.

Sinha, D.P.

1963a The Role of Paharia in Tribal Acculturation in a Central Indian Market. Ethnology, Vol. II.

1968b Culture Change in an Intertribal Market. Asia Publishing House, Bombay.

Sarma Thakur, G.C.

1976 Socio-economic Change in Post-Independence Period in a Tribal Village in Assam. The North Eastern Research Bulletin, Vol. III Summer.

Sahay, K.N.
1962 Trends of Sanskritization among the Oraon, Bulletin of Bihar Tribal Research Institute 2, Vol. IV.

Sachchidanand
1964 Culture Change in Tribal Bihar. Calcutta: Bookland Pvt. Ltd.

Schramm, W.
1964 Mass Media and National Development : The Role Information in Developing Countries. Stanford University Press, Stanford.

Spindler, G.D.
1955 Sociocultural and Psychological Process in Minomini Acculturation Berkeley : University of California Press.

Taske, Raymond H.C. Jr. and Bardin H. Nelson
1974 Acculturation and Assimilation : A clarification. American Ethnology 1 : 351-367.

Von Wiess, L.
1956 The Sociological Study of Social Change. Transactions of the Third World Congress of Sociology 1.

Vidyarthi, L.P. and B.K. Rai
1976 The Tribal Culture of India. The Concept Publishing Company, Delhi.

Vidyarthi, L.P.
1978 Rise of Anthropology in India. Vol. I, Concept Publishing Company, Delhi.

Wilson, Godfray and Monica H. Wilson
1965 The Analysis of Social Change : Based on Observations in Central Africa. Cambridge University Press.

Warner, W. Keith
1971 Structural Matrix of Development. In G.M. Beal, R.C. Powers and E.W. Coward Jr. (eds.), Sociological Perspective of Development. Ames: Iowa State University Press.

Weber, Max
1958 The Protestant Ethic and the Spirit of Capitalism. T. Parsons (Trans.), New York: Scrubners and Sons.

Warshay, Leon H.
1901 The Tribes of the Brahmaputra Valley. Reprinted 1975 by Sanskaran Prakashak, Delhi.

CHAPTER II

MISHINGS : A PORTRAIT OF THE TRADITIONAL SOCIAL SYSTEM

I

Assam is a land of numerous tribes having different ethnic and linguistic background. Since time immemorial, numerous tribes migrated to the Brahmaputra Valley (including the present hill States of North East India) and settled down permanently in this region. They mainly consist of the Indo-Austric (the Khasis), Dravidians (Kaibartas) and Mongoloid (Boro-Kachari, Naga, Chin-Kuki, Mishings and Arunachal Tribes). It is said that the tribes belonging to the Mongoloid stock of Tibet and Central China migrated to North-Eastern India and Assam along the Brahmaputra and its tributaries (Gait : 1905; Narzi : 1966). Several early British administrators had drawn vivid pictures of the tribes of Assam through their writings and monographs (M'Cosh :1837; Robinson : 1841; Hunter : 1879; Michell : 1883; Waddell : 1901; Gait : 1905; Endle : 1911; Baines : 1912).

There are various tribes in the hills and plains of present Assam. The major hill tribes of Assam are the Dimasas, the Mikirs (Karbi) and a few Naga and the Mizo tribes. Among the plain tribes, the Boro-Kacharis, the Kacharis, the Lalungs (Tiwa), the Deories, the Miris (Mishings) can be regarded as the major tribes. Their kinship system and social institutions differ from each other, even though, most of them have become Hindus (Gait : 1905; Devi : 1968; Dubey : 1977).

The following tables indicate the tribes of Assam in broad ethnic groups, their population, districtwise distribution of population, percentage to total population and increase in percentage during 1961-71.

Table 2.1

Scheduled Tribes Population in Assam[1]
(Based on 1971)

Tribes*	Total Population	Male	Female	P. C. to total tribal population
A. Boro-Kachari group				
Boro-Kachari	610,459	308,768	301,691	32.97

Kachari including Sonowal	198,619	102,547	97,072	10.74
Rabha	138,630	71,497	67,133	7.48
Barmans	18,210	6,761	6,449	0.71
Dimasa (Kachari)	39,344	20,713	18,631	2.13
Mech	2,570	1,276	1,294	0.15
Hajong	387	228	159	0.02
Lalung	95,609	48,397	47,212	5.16
Hmar	13,230	6,659	6,571	0.71
Hojai	2,298	1,135	1,163	0.12
B. *Kuki-Chin*				
Kuki group of tribes	21,034	11,150	9,884	1.14
Mizo (Luchai) group of tribes	242,689	4,294	4,201	13.12
Garo	9,161	5,243	3,918	0.49
Mikir (Karbi)	117,195	90,356	86,839	6.33
Chakma	22,789	12,015	10,774	1.23
Pawi	20,447	9,595	10,852	1.10
C. *Indo-Austric*				
Khasi and Jaintia	6,704	3,637	3,067	0.36
Synteng	611	305	306	0.03
D. *Indo-Tibetan*				
Miri (Mishing)	259,551	131,764	127,787	14.02
Deori	23,080	11,901	11,179	1.25
Man (Tai speaking)	964	489	475	0.05

1 Prepared with the help of Census of India, Assam State 1971, Part V : Special Tables, Ethnographic Notes on Scheduled Castes and Scheduled Tribes.

For socio-cultural purposes, few small groups of tribes/are included in broad ethnic groups which are more akin to them.

II

The Mishings are one of the major tribes of Assam. Their present population is 259,551 (Census, 1971). The tribe is settled mostly in the districts of Sibsagar, Dibrugarh, Lakhimpur, Darrang and Goalpara. Ethnically, they are Mongoloid and belong to the Indo-Tibetan group. Their ethnolinguistic affinity with Adis and Nishis of Arunachal Pradesh is striking

(Payengkataki : 1935; Pegu : 1956; Pamegam: 1972; Padun : 1972a; Doley : 1973; Bhandari : 1974). It is said that the Mishings migrated from the hills of Arunachal Pradesh into the plains of Assam about eight centuries ago and continued to do so till the first part of the nineteenth century.

Table 2.2

Districtwise Population of Scheduled Tribes, percentage to total population and percentage decade variation-1971

Districts	Total population	Percentage to total population in the district	Percentage increase during 1961-71
Goalpara	308,287	13.85	36.12
Kamrup	298,090	10.44	34.04
Darrang	185,640	10.69	32.32
Nowgong	125,115	7.44	42.93
Sibsagar	125,311	6.82	30.53
Lakhimpur	286,300	13.49	71.93
Mikir Hills	210,039	55.37	24.93
North Cachar Hills	52,583	69.75	21.71
Cachar	15,283	0.89	8.57

Source : Census of India, Assam State, 1971, Part V: Special Tables, Ethnographic Notes on Scheduled Castes and Scheduled Tribes.

Few years back, the Mishings were popularly known as Miris in the plains of Assam. How the Mishings have got the name Miri is a controversial issue. But it can be assumed that this name was given to them by the non-tribal Assamese people (Pegu: 1956:4; Pamegam: 1972:4). Among the Adis of Arunachal, the priest is known as *Miri* or *Mirin*. It is probable that non-tribal plains people of Assam called the tribe as *Miri* after they came into contact with the priests. Pegu (1956:5) is of the opinion that the *Mirin* (ghost), with its different forms, is generally led by the *Miri-Aboo* or *Myboo* or *Myiboo* (the functional titles of priests among the Adis). The *myiboo*, besides being the priest, acts as chronicler of the above tribes. As time eventually rolled on, they were bound to come in contact with the plains people of the Brahmaputra Valley who began to refer to their abode as the Miri Hills - the homeland of the Miris. This probably occurred more than six hundred years back as evident from the fact that *Mahapurusha* Sankardev (1449-1569 A.D.) and Madhavdev (1489-1566 A.D.), the two great Vaishnavite teachers and reformers had referred to the Miris in their devotional writings. Later on, the *Mishings* were popularly known as *Miris* in Assam. The meaning of the word *Mishing* is interesting. The members of the tribe regard themselves superior to other people. Therefore, they call themselves *Mi* (Men), *Yashing* (bright or good) = *Mishing*, which means "We are bright or good people", compared to the Mishings, and generally used for the people of the plains.

Since the invasion of the Ahoms on the Chutia Kingdom (1376 A.D.-1500 A.D.), the Mishings had relations with the plains people of Assam. When they came down from the northern hills, they came in close contact with the Chutias who had a kingdom around Sadia. When the Chutia kingdom was invaded and conquered by the Ahoms (1376 A.D.-1500 A.D.), it is said, a few nobles with their families took shelter in the Mishing villages and displayed feigned identity, as Mishing, to escape the disgrace of being molested by the Ahoms. Afterwards, matrimonial relationship between the Chutias and the Mishings took place. It is evident from the fact that few Mishing families still offer annual homage (*jal-pinda*) to some Chutia *Mine* (grand mother) in several Mishing villages. After cessation of the Chutia rule, the area around Sadia came under the administrative grasp of Sadia-Khowa-Gohain, a representative of the Ahom king. After a sporadic conflict, Sadia-Khowa-Gohain persuaded the Mishings to come to an agreement. According to that verbal treaty, the Mishings promised to help the Ahoms in resisting the other tribes who frequently attacked the Ahom border. To that effect twelve chiefs, or *Gams* (Boro-Gam), were appointed from some big Mishing villages and ten chiefs (*Dah-Gam*) from other villages. The *Gams* thus appointed, used to draw few hundred pieces of silver per annum from the Royal treasury of the Ahoms (Pegu: 1956). Thus, the Mishings have a distinct place in the Ahom history. Some of them held important military post as *Miri Hadinque* (Officer). Besides, the Ahoms giving recognition to the proficiency in displaying the bow and arrow, recruited many Mishings for their battalion of *Karhis* (archers). The Karhis played a magnificent part in the military operations of the Ahom kings. Some Mishing families belonging to the Pegu clan, still bear the title of Karhi-Pegu (Pegu: 1956).

The present site of Dibrugarh town was inhabited by a few Mishing villages till the British built their fort on the bank of the Dibru river, which eventually led to the formation of Dibrugarh town. The presence of Miri-Pather near Dibrugarh town bears testimony of it to this day (Pegu : 1956). The Mishings took active part in the Independence movement. Sahid Kamala Miri, who lost his life in the Independence movement, bears testimony of Mishing participation in the freedom movement. After the Independence of India, the Mishings have been recognised as a part of the Assamese community. Excepting their tribal customs and traditions, the Mishings are now-a-days a part of the regional Assamese culture through language, technique of production and polity.

III

As regards their deities, religious beliefs and practices, the Mishings regard the Sun (*Donyee*) and the Moon (*Polo*) as their ancestors. They regard the Moon as their father and the Sun as their mother. And therefore in any ritual performance, they first recite the name of *Ane' Donyee* (Mother Sun) and *Abu Po:lo* (Father Moon). As per their legends (Pegu, 1956:II), *Kiling-Kange* was the original abode of the Mishings (now in the Adi area of Arunachal Pradesh) from where they came down to *Regi-Regam* and spread to the South. On their way down from the hills, they were confronted with a rapid (*gili*) stream with extremely steep banks on either sides. Their efforts to cross the stream having failed, they began to worship the Sun (*Donyee*) and the Moon (*Po:lo*), their generators. One day, they found two huge creepers of golden colour (*Maying* and *Mankong*) growing by the bank, which, on cutting formed a bridge across the stream. These creepers they usually refer to as two golden ladders by which their forefathers came down from heaven (*Kiling-Kang*). *Shedi Babu* (Father Shedi) according to them, is the creator of all animates and inanimates. His predecessor - Pudolondo–the Divine one, emerged out of Infinity (*Tapapumang*). *Shedi Babu* first created the *Melo-Nane* (Mother Melo). All others on the earth are created by *Shedi Babu* and *Melo Nane*. Accordingly, the Mishings trace their clan organisation. Legends in this context are collected by Payengkataki (1935) around the rivers Siang and Subansiri of Arunachal.

IV

The Mishing villages are situated along the river courses of Upper Assam. The distribution of villages along the courses of the rivers Brahmaputra, Subansiri, Dishang, Dihing and their tributaries indicates the immigration of the Mishings. The Mishing villages are founded in a haphazard manner without proper planning. The front side of the houses generally faces the river. The houses of the Mishings are on piles, about 4 ft. to 5 ft. above the ground. The level for the floor is obtained from stilts. It may be made of wood or bamboo. On the stilts, they form the floor with the match of thick bamboo splits. The platform forms the main houses which is walled by mattings of split bamboo. The houses are about 40 ft. to 100 ft. in length and 10 ft. to 15 ft. in width. Several families usually dwell in a household, without a partition. For the bigger families several fire places are found, which indicate the size of the particular family. Various types of household utensils are used by the Mishings. The utensils are similar to the utensils of the non-tribal Assamese.

Social Life

The Mishings are peace loving people. Both men and women are hard workers. During the time of rituals and festivals, both enjoy as much as possible. The women are comparatively more hard working than men. They remain engaged in household and agricultural activities, and look after cattle breeding (pig and fowl), for extra income, from morning to evening. The members within the family follow the advice of the head of the family. Co-operation among the villagers is an important feature of the Mishings. *Rikbo-ge'nam* and *dagle'ka-ale'k* are some of their co-operative activities organized by a family whenever there is a need.

For instance, when a person is unable to cultivate his fields due to some reasons, he may request the villagers for co-operation (*rigbo gok nam*). To keep his request, the villagers will help him according to their capacity and time. For the construction of a new house, the owner may inform the villagers in advance and accordingly the villagers will help him.

The Mishings are divided into various groups though they do not strictly follow them. First they are divided into two broad divisions, viz., *Barogam* and *Dahgam*. These two are further sub-divided into *Pagro, Chayengia, Ayengia, Dambukial, Samuguria* and so on. Then, the clans of the Mishings can be categorised according to the sub-group. As for example, *Doley* and *Pegu* clans are normally included within *Pagro* sub-group and *Regon, Padun, Morang* are included within *Chayengia* or *Ayengia* sub-group. Matrimonial alliances are usually preferred within the sub-group. For instance, a man of *Doley* clan usually prefers to marry a woman of *Pegu* clan as both the clans belong to *Pagro* sub-group. Clan exogamy and sub-group and tribal endogamy is practised by them.

Clan and Kinship Organization

Clan organization of the Mishings is interesting from the sociological point of view. The Mishings trace their clan from the name of their forefathers or from the names of deities. According to their beliefs, there is a *Creator* of the Universe. They believe that the living beings of the world were created by a supreme being and therefore they trace their *Opi'n* (clan) from the name of that creator. According to them, the mystery prior to the creation of earth is the *Kooyum*. From the *Kooyum* six incarnations or evolutions took place. They were *Yumkang, Kashi, Shiang, Anbo, Bamuk, Muksheng* and *She:di*. Prior to *She:di*, which universal name is *Me:lo*, nothing was created in the universe. Later on, after the creation of *She:di* and *Me:lo*, several incarnations or evolutions took place. They were *She:di, Di ling, Li tung, Tu:ye, Yepe, Pe dong*. As they believe, the *Pe dong* is the *Supreme Creator* or *Mother* who created the Gods and Goddesses, human beings, animals, plants, insects and other creatures of this world. All the evolutions are regarded by them as deities. But the Mishings cite the name of *Mother Pe,dong* (mother rain) when they count their clan, because she is regarded as the creator of all.

Some of the Mishing clans are *Kuli, Kutum, Koman, Kagyung, Doley, Pegu, Pangging, Mo:do, Mo:rang, Mipun, Lagachu* and so on. The Mishings have sub-clans and clan-deity also. For instance, *Le:dang, Le:tung, Gejera, Patiri* are some of the sub-clans of *Doley* clan and their deity is known as *She:bo*. Clan-deities are not so important now-a-days in their social activities. There are few clans among the Mishings which came into being as a result of the contact with the Chutias, the Ahoms and the Bhuyans. Some of the Chutias took shelter in the Mishing villages when they were defeated by the Ahoms (1376 A.D.). Later on, they married Mishing women and became Mishings. The name *Chutia-Miri* or *Miri-Chutia* is the result of those inter-community marriages.

Like the Chutias, during the Ahom reign and the Burmese aggression, many Ahoms took shelter in the Mishing villages and settled down permanently. Hence, many Mishing families have adopted Chutia and Ahom surnames (e.g. Konwer, Handique, Gogoi, Gohain, etc.). The surnames are not regarded as clan names though they use them after their names.

Till the last part of nineteenth century, the Mishings did not use their clan name as surnames. At that time, the Mishings introduced themselves according to their father's name. Later on, the name of the father was regarded as the clan name and from then onwards clans have been playing an important role in all their social activities. Now-a-days, a man is not allowed to enter into the household if he does not know his own clan and clan-deity. Of course, it is not strictly followed by them.

Among the Mishings, the patriarchal joint family system is popular. However, a husband and a wife usually like to live together, separate from the main family. Within the patriarchal joint family, there are varying degrees of closeness in relationship. The relationships can be seen from kinship organization of the Mishings; the geneological pattern (see p. 23) shows the nature of their relationship.

It is seen that FaeBr, FayBr are regarded as *Babatta, Baboi* or *Apang*. Similarly, FaeBrWi and FayBrWi are regarded as mother of the ego. The relationship is consanguinal. To show the consanguinity *Kai* (Br), *Bi'ro* (Br), *Mamo* (BrWi), *Oi (Mo)* etc. are used. On the other hand if the relationship is affinial, the Mishings use *Magbo* (SiHu), *Yigo* (WiBr), *Yigne'* (WiSi) etc. The terms help to show two separate kinship groups in the geneological line. FaeSi and FaySi are known as *Abe'n Nyanyi* and *Amen Nyanyi* and their husbands as *Kake'*. One can marry FaeSiDa or FaySiDa or vice versa; similarly, MoeBrDa or MoyBrDa is allowed to marry by the ego which implies cross-cousin marriage. Levirate is also common among them.

The term *Yame'ng* is used for SoWi, eBrSoWi, yBrSoWi of the family. Once the term is used by a person, his relationship is regarded as affinial. He is allowed to come into matrimonial relationship with the SoWi's or eBrSoWi's families. The two terms *Magbo* (in case of senior) and *Yigo* (in case of junior) are used for FaSiSo, MoBrSo, HuBr, WiBr, SiHu and the two are affinial kinship terms. *Bi'-ro-birang* is used for Br, FaBrSo, MoSiSo, HuSiHu. Elder sister and younger sister are known as *Birme'*. Wife and husband are known as *Ne:ng* and *Milbong* respectively. Brother's wife is called *Amo/Mamo* (if elder) and *Yigne* (if younger). So BrSo, SiSo are known as *Ao*. The term *Eo* is used for BrSo (woman speaking), DaSo, HuSiSo, WiBrSo. *Ome* signifies Da, BrDa, SiDa and Dada.

Marriage

As mentioned earlier, the Mishings practise clan exogamy and tribal endogamy in their matrimonial system. Marriage within the same clan e.g., *Pegu* with *Pegu* or *Doley* with *Doley* will never be sanctioned. Similarly, marriages are restricted within the same sub-clan also. The cross-cousin marriage is common among them. The marriage is a relationship between two families. The individuals are secondary in a Mishing marriage. If a person marries his MoyBrDa or FaySiDa and vice-versa, both the ego's families, and his fa‹ner-in-law or mother-in-law usually

Relationship (Man speaking)

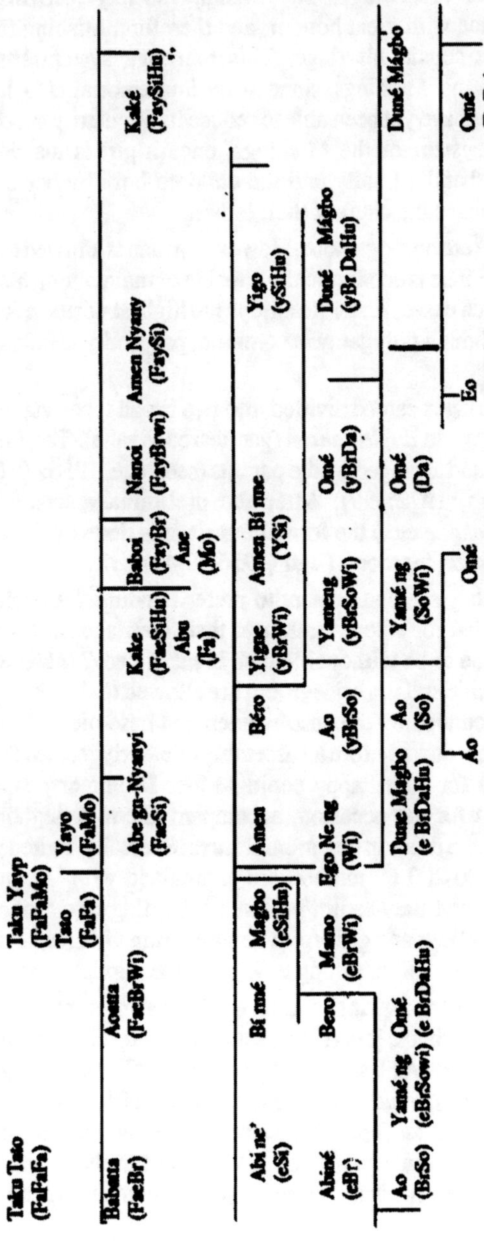

take it as a matter of prestige. The Mishing society recognises the matrimonial alliance with great honour, and therefore, Mishing families often prefer cross-cousin marriage. This marriage system has been prevailing among the Mishings since time immemorial. No modern acculturative forces have yet been able to reduce its popularity. According to the patrilineal system of the Mishings, once a girl is married, she belongs to her husband's family and the children born by her bear the surname (which means the clan) of their father.

The Mishings are monogamous. However, a man is allowed to marry more than one wife if he is economically capable of maintaining his wives and children. In such cases, first wife enjoys the highest position amongst the other wives. Though polygamy is common, polyandry is unknown to the Mishings.

Mishing marriages can be divided into two broad types viz. *midang* (arranged marriage) and *dugla-lanam* (gandharba vivaha). The first type is usually planned and arranged by the parents (see Pegu, 1956:40; Padun, 1972b:193; Regon, 1972:199). After the preliminary arrangements (*yame-tatnam, ar akune* etc.) the formal marriage is done by the parents of the bride and the bridegroom. Pegu (1956:40-41) writes:

> Though they seem at present to prefer Hinduism, a Brahmin is never called for solemnisation of their marriage. Instead a pig which need to be without blemish is sacrificed (*Makho-Basak*), and the bride and the bridegroom are allowed to dine in the same dish surrounded by the base-women and base-men. Finally the couple bow down before an assembly of elderly men and women who pray for their happy conjugal life. Drummers, especially appointed for the occasion, accompany them throughout, and they beat the drum in ceremonial ways. Specially invited guests, usually 100-200 in number, are entertained with 'Apong' and 'Ngosan' and they return presents according to their abilities. But young boys and girls from neighbouring villages, regardless of formal invitation, throng to witness the nuptial ceremony.

They join in merry-making, and on occasions volunteer to help the parties concerned. Perhaps, it is an expression of their fellow-feeling and reflection of their free and frank minds–so universal amongst the tribal people. In earlier days, a *mithun* or its equivalents of Rs. 100 or so was charged as *bride-price* (*alig*) payable to the bride's parents, but lately the amount has come to much variation and some families have totally abandoned the custom. The bride-price is a part of their custom rather than a demand of the parents of the bride in terms of dowry. Bride-price is usually taken in terms of damages done to the family (since a daughter helps to the family in economic activities). That is common in Gandharba Vivaha (*Dugla-lanam*) only. The practice is not an impact of the neighbouring non-tribal Hindus, but a traditional custom of their own. If we see from this point of view, *midang* (arranged marriage) is rather a product of the impact of the non-tribal Hindus. Because, the practice was not very much among the Mishings during the early period of their migration from the hills of Arunachal.

The other form of marriage which is still popular among them can be described as "Gandharba Vivaha" (*Dugla-lanam*) where the young couple concerned take the initiative. The young boys and girls working together in the fields, and dancing their ways in the *Porag* and *Aliailigang* festivals find an easy way for their childhood love to flourish, and if lucky enough their parents arrange for their final engagement. But if one of the parties disapproves the idea of their alliance or express inability to bear the expenses of a formal wedding, the boy by the help of his friends, takes away the girl on an appointed time and the bride is received in a little ceremony. The girl's parents are immediately informed and the matter is settled in a gathering known as *Orai-Binam*. In such cases, a higher bride-price is usually demanded though the total expenditure incurred in this system is usually less than in a *Midang*, and seems to be favoured by a considerable bulk of the population. Infant betrothal is known to be prevalent among them but the marriageable age is between 18-25 years for boys and between 15-20 years for girls. The divorce is allowed among the Mishings if conditions compel the couple for this. Widow re-marriage is also common among them. The widow is allowed to marry the younger brother of the deceased if she so desires. However, she cannot marry the elder brother of the deceased, who is regarded as a father figure.

Religion

The present religion of the Mishings is the synthetic product of animism and Hinduism. That religion among them is known as *Kewalia* or *Kalhanghati* or *Nishamlia*. Inspite of the mixture, they are worshippers of *Uyu* or spirit. The name of the *Donyee-Po:lo* (the Sun and the Moon) is recited in every ritual and festival. Some of the main *Pujas*-cum-festivals of the Mishings are *Po:rag, Ali-ai-ligang, Taleng Uyu* (pujas-cum-festivals concerned with agriculture), *Dabur, Ashi Uyu, Yumrang Uyu* (pujas for the deceased) and *Dodgang, Urom Apin* (pujas for ancestors or ancestor-worship). Thus the above pujas can be divided into three broad headings e.g. group puja, self or personal puja and pujas due to causes.

It has been mentioned earlier that the Mishings are the worshippers of numerous *Uyus* (spirits). In this context the *Miboo* (the priest) plays a significant role among them. He is supposed to know the *Uyus* responsible for all evil happenings of the Mishings. The *Miboo* usually offers chickens in the name of *Dopum-Dorum* (an imaginary spirit having three heads), and after some ritual activities the *Miboo* knows the measures for the remedy of the sufferer. Later, according to the direction of the *Miboo*, the family offers pig, fowl, *apong* etc. to the spirit for remedy.

One of the important rituals of the Mishings is the *Dobur-uyu*. The women are debarred from participating in it. During the performance of *Dobur-uyu*, traffic and business transaction with neighbouring villages is withheld for a day by constructing gates on both sides of the main entrance lane of the village. On the same day, the villagers approach each house demanding dues (*aje ng*). The families offer *apong*, pig, fowl and rice which they collect in the outskirt of the village.

> Two idols simulating the snake swallowing an egg, are prepared from some forn (*Tuktak*) and split bamboo and placed at the altar facing the rising sun. Pigs and fowls are sacrificed uttering some prayers meaning "Oh mother Sun, father Moon, Oh Divine Self, be pleased with these offerings and bless us with health and happiness, etc. (Pegu, 1956:57).

Dobur-uyu is performed once a year. This ritual is one of the examples of ritual performances of the Mishings. Due to the influence of Hinduism many changes have taken place in their religion and religious performances which will be discussed in details in Chapter V.

Festivals

There are various festivals performed by the Mishings. The most significant among them are the *Ali-ai-ligang* and *Po:rag*. They perform the three main *bihus* (festivals) of Assam, namely, the *Magh bihu*, *Bohag bihu* and *Kati bihu*, but the two festivals mentioned earlier are of their own. They perform them according to their traditional customs. Like their own traditional puja-cum-festivals, the Mishings perform *bihus* with equal enthusiasm. The three *bihus*, now-a-days, are regarded as a part of their culture. The Assamese *bihu* songs and Mishing *Oinitom* are equally popular among them. Both the Mishings and the non-tribal plains people are interdependent so far as the performance of *bihus* is concerned.

Formerly, the non-tribal plains people did not allow women to dance in *bihu* festivals. Now-a-days, by imitating the Mishings and other neighbouring tribes, they allow females to dance with men in festivals. This is one of the several influences of the tribal culture on the non-tribal population in the Valley. The adoption of *bihu* festivals by the Mishings can be regarded as the result of contact with the non-tribal plains people. *Ali-ai-ligang* or the spring dance festival is associated with agriculture, specially with the beginning of the *Ahu* paddy cultivation. The festival is celebrated on Wednesday of the month of *Falgun* of Indian calendar. The main objective of the festival is to pray to *Mother-Earth* for the production of *ahu* paddy. Before the festival, they clear up jungles for *jhumming*, manure the plot, erect new fencing and collect other necessary things for cultivation. On the auspicious day of the *Ali-ai-ligang*, they prepare food and drink in the forenoon and in the afternoon the heads of the families implant a handful of *ahu*-seed on their respective fields by reciting prayers to the Mother Earth. After that they offer few drops of *apong* in the four corners of the *me'ram* (fire-place) in their respective households. Then and there only they feast on food and drink. *Purang-apin* (packed boiled rice), *apong*, *adin* and *ango* are some of the main items of their feast. Later on, all villagers take part in a common feast.

In the festivals, young and old, irrespective of age and sex, join in merry making. A special dance known as *pakse-monam* is followed in which the indication of the movements of green leaves of *ahu* paddy, in different stages, are shown. The observance and the merry making associated with holidays of the *Ali-ai-ligang* continues for five days and they abstain during these days from all sorts of works. No work is generally allowed to be done in the *ahu* field, so that the Mother Earth shall be pleased and give them plenty of *ahu* paddy for their livelihood.

Another important festival, *Po:rag*, is also connected with agriculture. The festival marks the harvesting time of paddy which is celebrated with feasts and prayers. For the performance of *Po:rag*, *Murong* (dormitory) is essential. This festival has preserved the continuity of the *Murong* among the Mishings. The whole management of the festival falls on the shoulders of the *member-yame* (organization of young adults). Before the festival, a *Murong* is constructed, whose platform is 4 feet above the ground, and parallel to the river flow. After every preparation, a *Miboo* (priest) is appointed for prayer where *member-yame* of neighbouring villages are also invited.

The function starts with some offerings to the creator *Chedi-Melo* and *Donyi* (Sun), *Polo* (Moon) etc. with *Poro-Apong* procured by allowing water to drop through a meticulously prepared bamboo-cage (*Pobor*) full of the fermented materials. 4/5 pigs without a blemish are brought up specially for the occasion and are sacrificed. The days follow with prayers, feast and revelry, and the nights with prayer-dance (*Nitom-sumnam*), led by *Miboo*, dancing round in hops tightened to each other by cloth (Pegu, 1956:35).

The festival continues for three days and concludes with a prayer-dance (*ponu-nunam*).

Inspite of the two main traditional festivals and the *bihu* festivals, the Mishings engage themselves in various forms of merry-making. The hunting (*apta-ge' nam*) and fishing (*onge-ne'Knam*) are popular among them. These occasions are enjoyed by all villagers depending on their interests and physical fitness.

Folk Songs and Folk Dances

The Mishing folk songs are very interesting and meaningful. Though the songs are unwritten, they are surviving from generation to generation. As the other tribes of North East India, the Mishings are also very rich in folk songs. By studying the aims and objectives of the folk songs of the Mishings, Padun (1972 : 117) has divided them as follows:

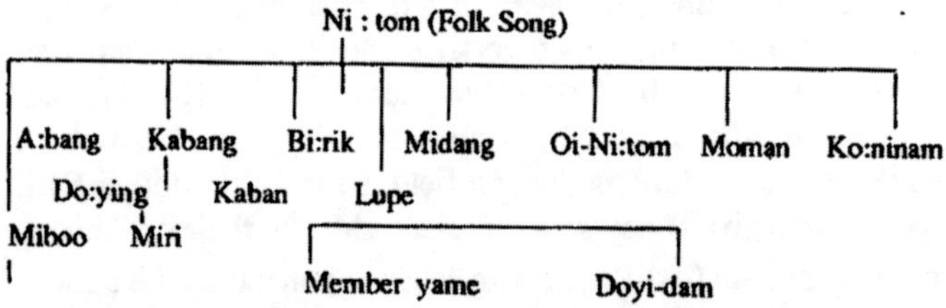

According to the above divisions, the folk songs of the Mishings can be divided into eight divisions. The first division A:bang, to a certain extent, is similar to classical songs. The language of the A:bang song is old and the song cannot be followed by ordinary people. It is generally used by the *Miboo* and *Miri* for ritual purposes. *Kaban* is just like an English ballad. They express their sorrows of the past and present through *Kaban* song. *Bi:rik* song is for seasonal festivals like *Ali-ai-ligang* and *po:rag*. Lupo is generally used as the expression of two persons and *Midang Nitom* is specially for marriage purposes only. The most popular song of the Mishings is *Oi-nitom.*

> This Oi-Nitom, which has an antique origin, is the outburst of their inner-most longings, a vent to appreciate the beauty of nature and thus it covers everything throughout their life, brings forth every conceivable reference where absorbing similies bloomsforth and unfold the throbbing story of their joys and sorrows (Pegu, 1956:48).

Moman nitom is for various games and merry makings and *Ko-ninam* to stop children from crying. This song is very popular among the Mishing women as they engage in household and agricultural activities with their newly born children tied on their backs.

The Mishing folk dances are allied in spirit and deliverance to the Bihu dance of non-tribal Assamese. Generally, pure form of Mishing dance (*Pagso monam*) is seen only in the festivals like *Ali-ai-ligang* and *Po:rag*. Both girls and boys with colourful dresses engage in dance in any festival. Along with the expression of musical instruments like *dhol, tal, pepa, dendum, tapungs, gungan*, the girls express the different stages of nature through their movements. *Oi-nitom* has played part and parcel of any type of dance and merry-making. The coloured dresses of the girls (e.g. ribi, gasing, egge, gero) and the boys (ugon, dumer, galuk etc.) in dance show the special production of weaving of the Mishing women (see Chapter V for elaborate discussion).

Political Life

The socio-political structure of the Mishings is democratic. Like the Pasi, Minyong and Padam of Arunachal Pradesh, the Mishings have *Ke'bangs* (Village Council) consisting of village elders within a village. The *Ke'bang* is supreme within a village which controls the social and political life of the villagers. Any complaint or anti-social activities are brought to the notice of it. The *Ke'bang* has the power to deliver judgments and punish the offenders. The punishment usually depends upon the nature of offence. Generally, it is in the form of the imposition of fines in money or kind, physical punishment or ex-communication. In case, controversy arises between two or more villages, *Bane-Ke'bang* or bigger *Ke'bang* is called for judgment. The *Gam* or now-a-days the *Gaonburah* acts as the chairman and delivers judgment in consultation with selected elderly villagers. Usually the women are not allowed to be a member of the *Ke'bang*.

The *Ke'bang* is held in the *Murong* where all discussions are taken by elderly villagers. The *Murong* or the public hall, though now-a-days found only in a few villages, is significant for community activities among them. Besides *Ke'bang*, the *member-yame* (young woman and man) is another village body consisting of members of younger age group. The body helps in all social activities within a village. The head or the Chairman of the *Member-yame* body is known as *Bora* who is responsible for the maintenance of the body.

Besides the above two important bodies, the Mishings have several other institutions which are responsible to maintain customary laws of the people which are there for all occasions, e.g. for marriage performance, divorce, widow-marriage, laws of inheritance and so on. These bodies, though smaller than the *Ke'bang*, work for the well being of the people within a village.

In conclusion, it can be said that the Mishings have a well organized social structure with tribal characteristics. But as they are living with the non-tribal Assamese for many centuries, changes have naturally been taking place in the tribal social structure.

References

Baines, Sir A.
1912 Ethnography. Reprinted 1976 by Concept Publishing Company, 65 F, Anand Nagar, New Delhi.

Bhandari, J.S.
1974 Land and Social Structure : An Economic Study of a Mishing Village. In S.K. Mathur and B.C. Agrawal (eds.), Tribe, Caste and Peasantry. Ethnographic and Folk Culture Society, U.P., Lucknow.

Devi, Lakshmi
1968 Ahom Tribal Relations (A political study). Cotton College, Gauhati.

Dubey, S.M.
1977 North East India A Sociological Study. Concept Publishing Company, New Delhi.

Doley, D.
1973 The Social-Economic Life of the Miri Tribe. North Eastern Research Bulletin, Vol. IV

Endle, S.
1911 The Kachari. Reprinted 1975 by Cosmo Publications, Delhi.

Gait, Sir Edward
1905 A History of Assam. Thacker Spink & Co. (1933) Pvt. Ltd. (Reprinted in 1967).

Hunter, W.W.
1879 A Statistical Account of Assam. Vol. II, Trubner & Co., London, Reprinted 1975 by B.R. Publishing Corporation, Delhi.

Michell, John

1883 The North East Frontier of India (a topographical political and military report). Reprinted 1973 by Vivek Publishing House, Delhi.

M'Cosh, John

1837 Topography of Assam. Reprinted 1975 by Sanskaran Prakashak, Delhi.

Narzi, Bhaben

1966 *Boro-Kacharir Samaj aur Sanskriti* (Assamese). Lawyers Book Stall, Gauhati.

Payengkataki, S.R.

1933 *Miri Jatir Buranji* (Assamese). Momoi Babejia, Dhemaji, Assam.

Pegu, N.C.

1972 *Miri ba Mishing*. In B. Kagyung (ed.), Mishing Sanskritir Alekhya, Birubari, Gauhati.

Padun, N.

1972a *Mishing Jana Jatir Parishay*. In B. Kagyung (ed.), *Mishing Sanskritir Alekhya*, Birubari, Gauhati.

1972b *Mishing Sakalar Baibahik Niti*, ibid.

1972c *Mishing Loka Sahitya*, ibid.

Regon, D.

1972 *Mishing Bibah Paddhati*, ibid.

Robinson, W.

1841 A Descriptive Account of Assam. Reprinted 1975 by Sanskaran Prakashak, Delhi.

Waddell, L.A.

1901 The Tribes of the Brahmaputra Valley. Reprinted 1975 by Sanskaran Prakashak, Delhi.

CHAPTER III

THE FIELD OF STUDY AND METHODOLOGY

In this chapter an attempt has been made to discuss the salient features of the field under study. The chapter is divided into two parts - the first part deals with the methodology of the study.

I

The present dissertation is based on the study of three villages. Keeping in view the requirement of the study, the three Mishing villages, i.e. Mohmora, Duhutimukh and Barpamua have been carefully selected. The selection of villages is based on purposive-random sampling. At the stage of the preliminary field visit to the Mishing area, it was found that the Mishing villages are situated either near the bank of the rivers of Upper Assam or in remote areas which lack regular contact and communication with the non-tribal population. Only a few villages are having regular modern system of communication and transportation. The main aim of this study is to understand and examine the impact of acculturation (contact with plains people, Hinduism, Assamese language, adoption of agricultural techniques and tools as applied by the non-tribal population), communication (post offices, telegraphs, telephone, newspaper, radio and the marketing centres) and the development (roads, rails, planning and community development) on the Mishings. The first two villages, Mohmora and Duhutimukh of Lakhimpur district are situated near the railway line and marketing centres in the midst of the plains Hinduised population. The third village, Barpamua is in Majuli sub-division of Sibsagar district. It is located in an isolated pocket, cut off from modern facilities of communication, but is better exposed to non-tribals, specially the Hindus as various religious monasteries (Satras) are situated in Majuli.

Location

The first village selected for study is Mohmora in Lakhimpur district of Assam. It is within the jurisdiction of Pub-Jonai Gaon Panchayat. The village is situated at a distance of about one kilometre from Jonai, a small town (now a sub-divisional headquarters) and about two kilometres from Murkongselek railway station which was constructed in the year 1964-65. The village is connected with the Oiramghat (ferry ghat) on the Brahmaputra, about five kilometres in the south-east direction. It is about 40 kilometres from Pasighat, sub-divisional town in Arunachal Pradesh. The motorable road (opened in 1960) passes through the village, connecting Jonai to Oiramghat. The village is well connected to Pashighat via Murkongselek railway station. The total area of Mohmora is 1246 *bighas* (1 acre is equal to 3 *bighas*). Generally the size of the land holdings of each individual family varies from 5 *bighas* to 10 *bighas*. The land holdings of a family consist 20 *bighas* to 100 *bighas* and above. One *Namghar* (Vaishnavite place of worship) and one *Murong* (dormitory) are there in the village. The village is composed primarily of two Mishing sub-groups, viz. *Moying* and *Pagro*.

Duhutimukh, the second village under study is within Dhemaji Gaon Panchayat. It is situated at a distance of about three kilometres from Dhemaji - the sub-divisional town of Lakhimpur district, and about five kilometres from Dhemaji railway station. The distance to Sonarighat, the ferry ghat on the Brahmaputra is about 18 kilometres from the village. The ferry ghat is connected with Dibrugarh town–the district headquarters. The motorable road connects the village with other areas. The village is situated haphazardly on both sides of the road. There is another newly constructed road across the village which connects the village with Dhemaji town.

The total area of Duhutimukh village is 851 *bighas*. The size of land holdings varies from 5 *bighas* to 50 *bighas*. There are no landless families in the village. There is one *Namghar* in the village but *Murong* is not there. The village is composed mainly of the *Moying* sub-group of the Mishings.

The third village under study is Barpamua in Majuli sub-division of Sibsagar district. Majuli is a river island of the Brahmaputra and is inhabited predominantly by the Mishings. The village is under Jengrai Gaon Panchayat. Barpamua is about 30 kilometres from Kamalabari, a small but important town of Majuli, and about 50 kilometres from Jorhat town—the district headquarters of Sibsagar (now Jorhat district). The village is situated on the bank of the river Khersuti, which makes the boundary between the Lakhimpur and Sibsagar districts. Jengraimukh, a marketing centre of Majuli is situated at a distance of only one kilometre from the village. The village is connected with the marketing centre by a river embankment. The nearest 'Satra'[1] (Vaishnavite monastery) is Garmurh which is at a distance of about 15 kilometres from Barpamua. Excepting in the summer season, Barpamua is well connected with the other parts of Majuli throughout the year.

The total area of the village Barpamua is 2680 *bighas*. The average size of land holding varies from 10 *bighas* to 20 *bighas*. There are no landless families in the village. There is one *Namghar* in the village and another *Namghar*, for the Bhagawatia villagers (another sect) is situated at a distance of one kilometre from the village. The village is composed primarily of the *Pagro* sub-group of the Mishings.

Historical Background of the Three Villages

The three villages have historical background of their own. The Mishings have a habit of dwelling near the banks of the rivers. Naturally, they have to shift from one place to another due to flood, erosion and other natural calamities. The three villages under study are not the original villages. They have grown out of shifts and resettlements. The following are the accounts of the history and settlements of these villages as narrated by a few knowledgeable persons :

According to Shri Brikuram Kumbang (age 55 years), the village Mohmora was situated in a small island of the Brahmaputra before 1950. The earthquake of 1950 had completely washed away the island and the villagers were compelled to shift from that place to the north bank of the river. They first shifted to *Bahir* Jonai in 1950 and stayed there for about three years. They shifted again from *Bahir* Jonai to Mohmora in 1954 and since then have been living at the present site of the village. According to Shri Jobalung Doley, another villager, the island, at that time, was regarded as the boundary between the NEFA and Assam. Shri Doley informed that the name Mohmora (place of the death of buffalows) was given by the villagers when a number of buffalows died due to unknown diseases during the course of their migration to the present village. Since then, the village is known as Mohmora. Some other villagers informed that one-fourth of the co-villagers migrated from different places to this village in search of economic security. The migrations and re-settlements are still continuing in the village. During the early fifties, the whole area was full of forests. The villagers transformed the area into cultivable land by hard labour and for that a significant number of co-villagers succumbed to unknown diseases. After a lot of suffering, the villagers settled down permanently in Mohmora.

The name of the second village, Duhutimukh has become popular as it was the source of two streams of the river Jiadhal in Dhemaji sub-division. This was told by Shri Dharmeswar Narah, one of the elderly villagers of Duhutimukh. According to him, in the beginning, the name of the village was Meruk, as the area was full of ashes of burnt out thatch. After that the village was known as Mukpi and finally in 1933 the village was renamed as Duhutimukh. Shri Narah informed that the Mishings are known for their migration from one place to another wherever and whenever it is felt necessary. In this case also, the villagers migrated from Majuli to Mashkhowa (near Dhakuakhana, about 25 kms from Duhutimukh) and then to Batua, and finally to the present village. The migration, according to him, took place during the early part of British rule in India. There are controversies among them about their original place. Shri Lamburam Kardong informed that most of the villagers are from Dihingmukh of Sibsagar district. The controversy is natural as the villagers migrated to the present village from different parts of Upper Assam.

The village Barpamua has the same background of migration as the earlier two villages. Shri Luchon Doley of Barpamua said that few families from Jhanji of Sibsagar district, first migrated temporarily to this village for *pam* (temporary settlement for cultivation). Later on, they found the place fertile and settled down permanently. Gradually, other co-villagers of the original village followed the former families. According to Shri Doley, he is not sure about the migration, but it was told to him by his grandfather. The migration could have taken place during the Ahom reign in Assam. Almost all the villagers are of the opinion that till 1950, the village was surrounded by deep jungles and chaparis (uncultivable waste land). The villagers settled down there with great difficulty. As a sign of these difficulties, there is a place known as Silosiko towards the eastern part of the village. During 1930-35, the villagers suffered heavily from cholera. In that critical situation, there was no one to bury the dead and the person who knew that his last breath was imminent went to that place and embraced death. Therefore, the place was known as Silosiko (the place of death by will). According to the villagers, this is an example of their hard days and their fight for survival.

From the accounts of the three villages, it is found that the villagers migrated from different places of Upper Assam to these villages. It is further proved that the Mishings are fond of migration (most probably for economic security) since time immemorial.

Demographic Composition

The three villages selected for study are within the predominantly Mishing area. All the villagers of Mohmora, Duhutimukh and Barpamua are Mishings except a few non-Mishing families. In Mohmora, one household belongs to a Marwari and two families belong to tea garden labourers, but their settlement is not permanent. In Duhutimukh, there are three permanently settled Bengali families. In the village Barpamua also one Bengali family and two Kaibarta (a Scheduled Caste community) families have settled permanently. Excluding these families, there are 106 households in Mohmora, 45 in Duhutimukh and 184 in Barpamua (1977).[2]

The total population of the three villages[3] is given in Table 3.1. It is significant from the table that in the three villages, the number of male is more than that of the female.

Table 3.1

Population of the three Villages

Sex	Villages and population		
	Mohmora	Duhutimukh	Barpamua
Male	396	195	645
	56.90	54.32	53.75
Female	300	164	555
	43.10	45.68	46.25
Total	696	356	1200
	100.00	100.00	100.00

Literacy

The people of the three villages under study are keenly interested in education. The literacy of the respondents of the villages of Mohmora, Duhutimukh and Barpamua is satisfactory. Adult education programmes and night school for the drop out children are operating in the three villages.

There is one L.P. School in Mohmora with an enrolment of 200 (140 boys and 60 girls) students. The M.E. School, which is situated at a distance of one kilometre from the village, has under its fold a total of 20 (10 boys and 10 girls) students. Two students are in college and there are three graduates in the village. In Duhutimukh, 60 (35 boys, 25 girls) students are in the village L.P. School, 30 (8 girls) students are in the H.E. School, 4 (1 girl) students are in the college. One post-graduate (M.A.) and 3 graduates are also there in the village. There are two L.P. Schools in the village Barpamua where 300 (100 girls) students from the village are enrolled. In the village, 50 (15 girls) students are studying in H.E. School, 8 are in college. There are one post-graduate (M.A.), 5 graduates, one M.B.B.S. and one diploma holder in Engineering in the village. All the three villages have been getting facilities of educational institutions from L.P. School up to college. In the case of Mohmora, the college is at Pashighat in Arunachal Pradesh, and the High School is at Jonai. They are only 20 kms and one km away respectively from Mohmora. The High School and the college at Dhemaji are only 3 kilometres away from the village Duhutimukh. Similarly, Jengraimukh High School and college and other institutions are at a distance of only one kilometre from Barpamua village.

II

The villages for the present study are selected by random sampling method. For the formulation of the hypothesis which is mentioned in the first chapter, the research design[4] of the present study is prepared as simple as possible. The study is based on participant observation, informal discussion and the administration of a Structured Interview Schedule. The following techniques were adopted to collect the data :

1. Village Schedule : General data about the field of study (Schedule I).
2. Household Schedule (Schedule II).
3. Case Studies : legends, history and statement of the older persons (Schedule III).
4. Interview Schedule (Schedule IV).

Village Schedule (Schedule I)

To collect general data of the three villages under study, a detailed village schedule was prepared. The village schedule was helpful in collecting systematic data and information regarding the location of the village, myths, legends and historical accounts associated with the villages, households, population, sex composition, acculturation, including important points on religion, food-habits, language, housing pattern, dress, tools and implements, clan and kinship organizations, communication, roads, railways, marketing centres, post and telegraph, radio, newspaper, development activities in pre and post independence period, agriculture, economy, income, health and education.

Household Schedule (Schedule II)

We wanted to collect complete information about the Mishing families living in these villages with special reference to the nature of the family, size of the family, size of the landholdings, occupations and income of the different members of every household, marital status, educational status etc. For this purpose we took the help of two methods:

(a) Household Schedule

(b) Informal interviews and participant observation.

Actually, the questions related to household were included within the interview schedule (Schedule IV) and both schedules were combined together.

Keeping in view the complexities of social customs, cultural norms and values of the Mishings, the investigator, specially gave stress on participant observation and informal interview. Because variations are common in social activities of the Mishings in various parts of Assam. During the time of preliminary field visit, adequate attention was paid to collect relevant facts by participating in the day-to-day life of the villagers. In the field diary, all relevant facts were noted down.

As in the preliminary field visit, during the time of extensive field work, sufficient attention was paid to participant observation, which is a reliable technique for proper understanding of the society. To have a proper knowledge, the investigator took part in the daily evening gossips of the villagers, took meal with them, participated in the meetings held for the settlement of village disputes and in rituals and *pujas*. When the investigator was in Mohmora village, it was summer. He took part in the activities of the paddy field where paddy cultivation was going on. In Barpamua, it was a rewarding experience to share the sorrows and sufferings of the flood affected, economically downtrodden villagers. After taking part in all activities with the villagers, special attention was paid to write regular notes in the field diary where the observations were recorded carefully.

Case Studies (Schedule III)

To make the present study useful and authentic, special emphasis was laid on in depth case studies to focus the attention on some specific points. The case studies are both qualitative as well as quantitative. These case studies throw light on historical accounts, customs, practices in previous generation, and entrepreneurship. In the course of discussion, while using the technique of case studies, we tried to know about social and cultural affairs, economy, mass media and education as prevailing among the Mishings.

Interview Schedule (Schedule IV)

The Interview Schedule was prepared with simple questions, keeping in view the main objective of the present study. The direct questions in the form of table were included in the Schedule. The special attention was paid to ensure accuracy, proper communication and appropriate response from the respondents. The Interview Schedule included questions on household data also. The Schedule was divided into five broad divisions. The personal background, family background, acculturation, communication and development were the broad divisions in the Schedule. Altogether 64 questions were included in the Schedule. The questions were selected carefully with an eye on the needs of the study. The main intention behind the use of Interview and Household Schedules was to collect essential data on the respondents and their households with special emphasis on the age, sex, educational qualification, income, nature of family, size of family. Secondly, the questions related to acculturation in religion, food habit, language, house pattern, dress and household utensils were also included in these Schedules. The questions on communication and development were prepared to collect data on mass communication, occupations, improved agricultural tools, medical aids, education for the children of the respondents and opinion in connection with the development of their community.

The Interview Schedule was tested on a sample of Mishing students within the University campus. In the light of the experiences of the pre-testing, the necessary modifications were made in the Schedule and it was found suitable after the pilot study and modification for field study. The Schedule was translated from English into Assamese. Then it was given to the press for printing.

Establishment of Rapport

The respondents showed enthusiasm in the study and helped the investigator in all possible manner. It was not difficult to establish rapport with the respondents because the investigator belongs to the same community and speaks their dialect. Keeping in view the probable complexities, the respondents were allowed to use narrative form, least interrupted by the investigator.

During the course of discussions and preparation of the case study, the respondents were given every freedom to narrate incidents and their feelings. The field work was conducted during the summer. It was a matter of pleasure that in spite of so much busy time in cultivation during day-time, the respondents eagerly participated in discussion at night. It was found that the respondents were proud of being the Mishings and they were much conscious about their identity.

Field Experience

During the course of field work, a lot of problems were faced by the investigator. The most serious problem was the inadequacy of roads and drains within the villages. The whole Mohmora village was flooded due to heavy rains and it was very difficult to move from one house to another at the time of field work. It was difficult even to contact the respondents outside their houses as they did not like to get down from *chund ghar* (house on pile). The same was the case in the village Duhutimukh and village Barpamua also.

The Mishings still believe in superstitions. This impression was strengthened when the field work was going on in Barpamua village. A fishery was poisoned by someone nearby that village, due to which the fishes died. When it was difficult to find out the culprit, the villagers of that area circulated a notice of warning by saying that if the culprit would not confess himself, the villagers will perform a ritual by sacrificing two pigs and by cutting a banana tree which shall incur death to the culprit. When the investigator asked about the probable effect of the ritual, one of the villagers told 'wait and see the result'. Earlier one person succumbed to that type of ritual as he did not confess his crime, as informed by the villagers.

Classification, Tabulation and Editing

After the completion of the field work, the first step was the editing, classification and tabulation of the village schedules, household and interview schedules and case studies. The editing was done carefully. The data provided by the Schedules were classified carefully for tabulation, e.g. age and sex, education and income and so on.

The tabulation was done after completion of the classification. It has already been mentioned that classification was done according to the Schedule. The tables included in this study are simple. They have been prepared to make the purpose clear, to make significance clear, to express the data in the least space and to make comparison easy. The tables are classified mainly into two types, viz. general purpose tables and summary tables. The aim of the general purpose table or reference table is to have a general information regarding the whole collected data, such as age group and marital status of the respondents, educational qualifications and annual income of the respondents, a few tables are comparative, for example, family size and family income of the respondents. Every possible care was taken to make the tables objective and clear. For that purpose editing was done at every step of classification and tabulation.

Identification of Variables

It has already been mentioned in the introduction chapter that the main aim of this study is to see the impact of the two independent variables - acculturation and communication on the dependent variable 'development'. 'Acculturation' includes the impact of Hinduism on Mishing's religion and changes in food-habits, language, housing pattern, dress and tools and implements of the Mishings. In the field of communication, attempt has been made to see the traditional Mishing communication system. Prior to the migration of the Mishings from the hills of Arunachal to the plains of Assam, oral communication was prevalent among them. After migration to the plains of Assam, they adopted other methods of communication. The learning of Assamese language, writing and the use of mass-media were gradually adopted by them. For the study of communication, these factors have been taken into consideration. The special care has been observed to see as to how the gradual changes in communication system, along with the other agencies, have been helping in the development of the Mishings. Gradual development started after the improvement of road transportation and railways. As a result of the growth of the marketing centres, they started producing surplus agricultural products for marketing purposes. To increase production, they adopted new technology and methods such as tractor, chemical fertilizer, irrigation, use of high yielding seeds in their cultivation. Due to the marketing centres, money economy started among them and as a result, they became a part of the regional, national and the world economy. These changes are conducive in the development of the Mishings. After considering these factors, the relevant variables were identified for this study.

Analysis

The analysis of the preceding chapters is based on logical as well as statistical analysis. The assumptions and hypotheses of this study are based on theoretical discussions as presented in the first chapter. The statistical analysis is based on tables prepared on the basis of primary and secondary data. In each chapter, case studies are included to substantiate the main point and make in-depth analysis of a focused problem.

Chapter Scheme

After the preparation of the primary and secondary data and the proper allocation of the tables, chapter scheme was prepared for this study. The following is the chapter scheme:

(a)	Chapter - I	Introduction.
(b)	Chapter - II	Mishings : A Portrait of the Traditional Social System.
(c)	Chapter - III	The Field of Study and Methodology.
(d)	Chapter - IV	Social Background of the Respondents.
(e)	Chapter - V	Acculturation among the Mishings.
(f)	Chapter - VI	The Communication.
(g)	Chapter - VII	The Socio-economic Development.
(h)	Chapter - VIII	Overview and Concluding Remarks.

References

1. The *Satras* (monasteries) are Vaishnavite religious institutions of Assam. These institutions played crucial roles in the propagation of Vaishnavism in this State. The Aonihati Satra, Kamalabari Satra and Garmur Satra of Majuli are famous and popular among the Vaishnavas of Assam.
2. Two groups of villagers of Barpamua had migrated from the village to form two small villages. One is about two kilometres from Barpamua and now having a separate identity in all activities from the original village. Therefore the household of that village is not included here. Another group has settled down near Jengraimukh Bazar and all village activities are performed according to what was done in the old village, so they are included in this study.

3. The Gaon Panchayats (Pub Jonai G.P., Dhemaji G.P. and Jengrai G.P.) records of 1975 have been found wrong in course of my field work. The household and population data given here are collected by household schedules and participant observation. The total household and the total population figures supplied by the Gaon Panchayats of the respective villages have therefore been not given here.
4. See C. Selltiz, M. Johoda, M. Deutsch & S.W. Cook (eds.), Research Methods in Social Relations. Methuen & Co. Ltd. 11 New Fetter Lane, E.C. 4. 1965.

Babechuk, Nicholas

1962 The Role of the Research as participant observer and participant-as-observer in the field situation. Human Organisation 3, Vol. 21.

Bruyn, Severyn

1963 Methodology of Participant Observation. Human Organisation 3, Vol. 22.

Goode, W.J. and P.K. Hatt

1952 Method in Social Research. McGraw-Hill Kogakusha Ltd., Tokyo.

CHAPTER IV

SOCIAL BACKGROUND OF THE RESPONDENTS

This chapter throws light on the social background of the respondents. The main focus of this chapter is on the following points:

(a) The age and the marital status of the respondents;

(b) Education of the respondents;

(c) Size of the family and income; and

(d) The nature of the family.

Age Group and Marital Status of the Respondents

The Mishings are monogamous. It has been mentioned in the earlier chapter that clan exogamy and tribal endogamy are practised by them. Both arranged marriage (*Midang*) and *Gandharba vivaha* (*Dukla-lanam*) are common among them.[1] The latter marriage system is more popular than the former. Early marriage is preferred by the Mishings though some of the educated persons, now-a-days, prefer late marriage.[2] Divorce, widower and widow re-marriage are allowed among them. In this respect, they must fulfil the norms of the *Kebang* (Village Council). Table 4.1 shows the age group and marital status of the respondents.

It has been found that out of 335 respondents, 300 (89.57%) are married, 10 (2.98%) are unmarried, 16 (4.77%) are widows, 5 (1.49%) are divorced. Out of the 300 married respondents, 61 belong to the age group of 31-35, 24 respondents are within the age group of 46-50. All unmarried respondents (10) are within the age group of 30. The mean age of the respondents is 43 years. Within age group of 41 to 45, there are 16 (13.73%) respondents. Out of them, 34 are married, 8 are widows, 2 widowers and 2 are divorced. Out of the 335 respondents, 317 (94.63%) are male and 18 (5.37%) are female.

Among the Mishings, generally the marriages are held after attaining maturity. As regards the opinion on the early marriage, the size of family and economic conditions, the following case studies throw sufficient light.

Table 4.1

Age Group and Marital Status of the Respondents

Age Group	Marital Status					Total	Mid value	Fi.xi	Mean
	Married	Unmarried	Widowl	Widower	Divorce	(fi)	(xi)		$\frac{fi.xi}{fi}$
Up to 30	36 78.26 12.00	10 21.74 100.00	—	—	—	46 13.73	28	1288	
31-35	61 100.00 20.33	—	—	—	—	61 18.22	33	2013	$\frac{14510}{335}$
36-40	48 88.89 16.00	—	6 11.11 37.50	—	—	54 16.12	38	2052	43 yrs. (Mean age)
41-45	34 73.91 11.33	—	8 17.39 50.00	2 4.35 40.00	2 4.35 50.00	46 13.73	43	1978	
46-50	24 85.72 8.00	—	1 3.57 6.25	1 3.57 20.00	2 7.14 50.00	28 8.36	48	1344	
51-55	28 93.33 9.33	—	1 3.33 6.25	1 3.33 20.00	—	30 8.95	53	1590	
56-60	32 96.97 10.66	—	—	1 3.03 20.00	—	33 0.85	58	1914	
Above 60	37 100.00 11.21	—	—	—	—	37 11.04	63	2331	
Total	300 89.57	10 2.77	16 1.49	5 1.49	4 1.19	335 100.00		14510	

Mean fi$\frac{xi}{fi}$, where fi means frequency and xi means mid value

Case Study 4.1

Name–Shri Ganesh Doley, age–50 years, size of family–5, number of children–4, size of landholding–49 *bighas*, annual income–Rs. 2,000.00, number of children going to school–1. Village–Mohmora.

Shri Ganesh Doley revealed a number of points on marriage, economy and education of his family. He did not support early marriage of his children although it was the usual practice in the village. According to him, due to poor economic conditions he found it hard to educate his children. But it did not mean that they should get married at an early age. There is no need for a large family, now-a-days, as cultivable land is limited. His present land for cultivation is hardly sufficient to meet the requirements of his family members. Therefore, he does not prefer more members in his family.

Case Study 4.2

Name–Shri Moheswar Narah, age–52 years, size of family–14, number of children–8, size of landholding–16 *bighas*, annual income–Rs. 3,500, number of school going children–8, other source of income-younger brothers are in government service and business.

Shri Narah of Duhutimukh village is in support of the late marriage in case of boys and early marriage in case of girls. He is not in favour of birth control. According to him, "I am in favour of late marriage for boys, because they should marry only after they are properly established in life. But birth control is not necessary as more population is required for the growth and expansion of Mishing community all over Assam".

Education of the Respondents

The percentage of literacy among the Mishings was only 18.20 in 1971 (Mipun, 1976 : 175). In the post-independence period, concerted efforts have been made for educational development among the tribes. No doubt, tribals of India have been given special facilities right from the primary stage to the University stage. But the tribals are still educationally backward, though in case of tribal education, position in Assam is slightly better (Vidyarthi and Rai, 1977 : 444). The following table shows the level of education of the respondents :

Table 4.2

Educational Level of the Respondents

Educational levels	Total	Percentage
Illiterate	130	38.80
Literate	162	48.37
Under Matric	33	9.85
Matriculate and above	10	2.98
Total	335	100.00

According to the above table, even though 130 (38.80%) respondents are illiterate, the rest (67.20%) are literate.

The sons and daughters are comparatively more educated than the respondents. The highest literary standard among the literates is up to L.P School. All the literate persons are able to read and write Assamese language. The person with the highest education among the respondents is an M.A. of Barpamua village. His case study is as follows :

Case Study 4.3

Name - Shri Indreswar Pegu, age–45 years, land–24 *bighas*, income–Rs. 1,500 P.M. (approx.), other source of income–business.

Shri Pegu of Barpamua village is the Principal of Jengraimukh College. He was motivated to higher studies by imitating the non-tribals. When he passed the Matriculation examination, there were few qualified Mishing persons in his area to guide him for higher study. He supported his education mainly by doing petty business and working in temporary services. He appeared in college and University examinations as a private candidate. He was from a poor family. Therefore, he is satisfied with his present achievements. He wants to be a pioneer social worker for the development of the Mishing community. He is not only a Principal of a College, but at the same time, a cultivator, writer, composer of Mishing songs and religious preacher of the Bhagavatia Sect.

Annual Income

Cultivation is the primary occupation of the respondents of the present study. Inspite of the landholdings, the economy of the Mishings is not sound. It is because of lack of adequate cultivable land, constant floods and erosions in the Mishing populated areas. Moreover, one of the predominant factors, as indicated by Doley (1973 : 61) and Bhandari (1974 : 19), is the impact of customs which are non-economic in nature. Still then the annual income of the respondents of the present study is satisfactory. The mean annual income which is given in the table below was beyond the imagination of the respondents when they first migrated to these villages. It took several years for them to be self-sufficient in agricultural productions and domestic possessions.

Table 4.3

Annual Income of the Respondents

Income Group	Total	Mid Value	Fi.xi	Mean $\frac{fi.xi}{fi}$
Up to 1500	95 28.56	1250.5	118797.5	
1501-2000	44 13.14	1750.5	77022.0	$\frac{fi.xi}{fi}$
2001-2500	50 14.92	2250.5	112525.0	$\frac{819417.5}{335}$
2501-3000	58 17.31	2750.5	159529.0	2556.02 (Mean Annual Inome)
3001-3500	13 3.88	3250.5	42256.5	
3501-4000	19 5.67	3750.5	71259.5	
Above 4000	56 16.72	4250.5	238028.0	
Total	335 1.00.00		819417.5	

*Mean = $\frac{fi.xi}{fi}$ where fi = frequency, xi = mid value.

The above table shows that 95 (28.36%) respondents are in the income group of Rs. 1500.00 and 56 (16.72%) are above the income group of Rs. 4000.00. 13 respondents (3.88%) are found in the income group of Rs. 3001.00 to Rs. 3500.00. Other 44 (13.14%) respondents are within the income group of Rs. 1501 to Rs. 2000, 50 (14.92%) are within Rs. 2001 to Rs. 2500, 58 (17.31%) are within Rs. 2501 to Rs. 3000 and 19 (5.67%) are within the range of Rs. 3501 to Rs. 4000. The mean annual income of the respondents is Rs. 2446.02.

A few of the respondents have additional sources of income. Small shop keeping, part time business are the usual additional sources of income of the villagers. We have tried to understand the economic position of a few families in details by collecting case studies of two persons having the largest and the lowest landholdings among the respondents. Further, we have made case study of a person whose family has more than one source of income.

Case Study 4.4

Name–Shri Mohiram Doley, age–55 years, family members–12, land–60 *bighas*, annual income–above Rs. 4000.00.

> The economic condition of Shri Mohiram Doley of Mohmora village is sound. His major agricultural products are paddy, black pulse, mustard and vegetables. The surplus agricultural products are sold in the market for extra income. His income is sufficient to maintain his family. His younger son is a commerce graduate. The grandsons and grand daughters of Shri Doley are going to schools. At present, sufficient savings are made by him, but no accounts are maintained in the family. The savings are spent in purchasing agricultural tools and implements and in meeting expenses of the school going grand sons and daughters.

Case Study 4.5

Name–Shri Bhugeswar Narah, age–38 years, family members–5, land–3 *bighas*, annual income-below Rs. 1500.00.

> Having only 3 *bighas* of land, Shri Narah of Duhutimukh village has to maintain his family by doing daily labour. During the summer season, he works as halua (plough man) for three to four months in a well-to-do family of his village. He is paid both in cash and kind. His patrons helped him in his hard days, specially in the season when no works are available in the village. Due to his poor economic condition, he is not in a position to send his brother and sons to the school.

Case Study 4.6

Name–Shri Monidhar Taye, age–55 years, family members–6, size of landholding–45 *bighas*, annual income above Rs. 4000.00.

> Shri Taye of Mohmora village has various sources of income in addition to agricultural productions. He is the owner of a small shop and a truck. He states : "It is difficult to depend only on agricultural productions. For sound economic condition of a family, additional sources of income apart from agricultural productions are essential.The sound economic condition of my family has helped in my participation in all social, economic and political activities in the area". All his sons and daughters are studying in schools. He desires to give them higher education.

It is worthwhile to see the income according to the size of the family. Being cultivator, the economy of Mishings depends on the size of the family and the man power. The larger is the number of family members, the higher is the accumulated income of the family. Almost in all extended families, few members are engaged in petty business such as shop keeping, contract, milk business etc. and some of the members are in services also. All the income of the family members is usually handed over to the head of the family, and ultimately the income of the family is enhanced. Table 4.4 indicates the income of the respondents according to the size of the families.

Family Size and Income of the Respondents

Table 4.4 shows that there are 26 families with 15 members and of them 12 (14.17%) families are in the income group of above Rs. 4,000.00. Within the family size of 10-12, income of the 6 (10.34%) families are Rs. 1,500.00, out of the total 58 families of the same family size, income of the 15 (25.88%) respondents are above Rs. 4,000.00. In the smallest family size of 3, income of the 21 (75.00%) families are below Rs. 1,500.00. As mentioned earlier, it is seen from the table that the income of the family essentially depended on the size of the family. The figures of the table prove our statement.

On the basis of the figures of table 4.4, the following findings can be derived:

(a) There is a relationship between the size and the income of the family. The large families are found to be having the higher income.

(b) In the larger families, there are additional sources of income. Though cultivation is the main source of livelihood and income, some of the members of the larger families are found to be engaged in business and contract.

Table 4.4

Family Size and Income of the Respondents

Size of Family	Income Group						Above 4000	Row Table
	Up to 1500	1501-2000	2001-2500	2501-3000	3001-3500	3501-4000		
Up to 3	21 75.00 22.00	—	7 25.00	—	—	—	—	28 100.00
4 – 6	45 45.46 47.37	17 17.17 38.64	15 15.15 30.00	10 10.10 17.24	6 6.06 46.15	—	6 6.60 10.71	99 100.00
7 – 9	23 25.02 24.21	17 18.47 38.54	13 14.13 26.00	21 22.83 36.22	—	7 7.60 36.86	11 11.95 19.64	92 100.00
10 – 12	6 10.34 6.32	10 17.24 22.72	8 13.79 16.00	13 22.41 22.41	—	6 10.34 31.57	15 25.88 26.79	58 100.00
13 – 15	—	—	7 21.87 14.00	6 18.75 10.34	7 22.87 53.85	—	12 37.51 21.43	26 100.00
Above 15	—	—	—	8 30.76 13.78	—	6 23.07 31.57	12 46.17 21.43	26 100.00
Column	95	44	50	58	13	19	56	335
Total	100.00	100.00	100.00	100.00	100.00	100.00	100.00	100.00

Nature and Size of Family

A Mishing family consists of spouses and their unmarried children. Though the respondents are in favour of extended family for agricultural activities and for economic security, the newly married couple usually prefer to live separately from their parents. In some cases when one of the spouses dies, the widow or widower lives with the unmarried children and they rarely share the residence with the married son or daughter. In extended families, the parents and their sons and daughters live together. In such families, the father of the married son will be the head of the family. The following table shows the nature and size of family of the respondents.

Table 4.5

Nature and Size of Family of the Respondents

Nature of Family Member	Size of Family Large Family	 Small Family	Total (fi)	Mid value (xi)	Fi. xi	Mean= $\frac{fi.xi}{fi}$
Up to 3	—	28 100.00 22.05	28 8.36	2	56	
4-6	—	99 100.00 77.95	99 29.55	5	495	Mean= $\frac{fi.xi}{fi}$
7-9	92 100.00 44.23	—	92 27.46	8	736	$= \frac{2789}{335}$
10-12	58 100.00 27.88	—	58 17.32	11	638	= 8 (Mean Family Size)
13-15	32 100.00 15.38	—	32 9.55	14	448	
Above 15	26 100.00 12.51	—	26	16	416	
Total	208 62.09	127 37.91	335 100.00		2789	

A few of the case studies made in this regard focus our attention on the question of the nature and the size of the family. The economic compulsions are having their impact on the tribal mind and they are thinking in terms of smaller family which is manifested by the following case study :

Case Study 4.7

Name–Shri Debeswar Pegu, age–50 years, family members–5, Majuli, the river island of the Brahmaputra, suffers constantly from floods and erosions. Recollecting the hard days, Shri Pegu an old villager of Barpamua in Majuli, said : "I have lost my confidence now-a-days to talk about our economic conditions. It is painful to recollect those prosperous days before the great earthquake of 1950. After the earthquake, we have been losing everything due to constant floods and erosions. Our economic condition is no longer sound. Therefore, I feel the need of a small family rather than an extended one. The smaller family offers better opportunity for education and future of our children."

Almost all the villagers under study were of the same opinion. It may be contrary to their expressed eagerness for a larger Mishing community, but they are in favour of the opinion as expressed above. They are found to be keenly interested in education of their children and feel that their future prospects depend on education.

References

1. See N.C. Pegu, *The Miris or the Mishing of the Brahmaputra Valley*, Kumarbari, Majuli, Assam, 1956, pp. 38-41 ; N. Padun, *Mishing Sakalar Baibahik Niti*, pp. 193-98 in B. Kagyung (ed.), *Mishing Sanskritir Alekhya*, Birubari, Guwahati, 1972; D. Regan, *Mishing Bibah Paddhati*, pp. 199-207, in *ibid;* B. Kagyung, *Dugla Lanam*, pp. 207-13 in *ibid*.
2. The age group of the married respondents is much higher as shown in the table. But the respondents informed that their married life started at the age group of 20-25. Even today, some of them prefer the same age group for marriage of their sons.

CHAPTER V

ACCULTURATION AMONG THE MISHINGS

I

The process of cultural contact and interaction between the tribes and the non-tribes, and between the little and the great tradition (Redfield : 1955) is not a new phenomenon in Assam. The tribes of North-East, in the traditional Indian Texts were called 'Kirata' (Borua: 1951; Chaterji : 1951). As indicated in the Mahabharata, their King Bhagadatta participated in the War at Kurukschetra. Historically, this area was ruled by Varman (4th to 8th Century A.D.), Pal (11th to 12th Century A.D.), Baro Bhuyan (12th to 13th Century A.D.), Chutia (13th to 16th Century A.D.), Ahom (13th to 19th Century A.D.), Koch (16th to 17th Century A.D.), and Kachari (16th to 19th Century A.D.) dynasties (Gait : 1905). Ethnically, most of these dynasties belonged to the different tribal communities which were Hinduised in the course of time through cultural contact and interaction (Dubey : 1978).

To understand the nature of acculturation among the Mishings, we shall have to keep in mind three phases of their socio-cultural life. In the first phase, they were hill dwellers in the Adi Area of today's Arunachal Pradesh. At the second phase, they moved to the plains of Assam. At the third phase, they came in contact with their neighbours and adopted their religion (Hinduism), language (Assamese) and polity. After their migration to the plains, the Mishings developed interaction with other tribes (Kacharis, Mikirs, Boro-Kacharis) and Castes (Hinduism, Assamese population). The process of cultural interaction may be explained in terms of the growing relationship between the macro (tribal isolated villages), middle (regional economy, culture and polity) and micro (mythology, beliefs, worship, ideology and caste system) levels.

To analyse the process of acculturation, we can take the help of the theoretical framework as explained through the concept of the dominant and the weak cultures (Mead : 1932, Herskovitz : 1938) and the little and great traditions (Redfield : 1955).

(a) As explained by Mead and Herskovitz, the contact between the dominant and the weak cultures leads to the disorganisation of the religious practices and the traditional life styles of the latter. It creates marginality among the members of the weak çulture.

(b) In certain situations, the people belonging to the weak culture, try to find out the common elements between their culture and the dominant culture.

(c) As pointed out by Redfield, the interaction between the little community (tribes), peasant societies and great traditions (elite languages, mythology and organised religion) leads to acculturation which breaks the isolation, self-sufficiency and homogeneous nature of the little community.

The above theoretical framework provided a base for our analysis. In this chapter, our main focus is on the following points :

(a) What changes occurred among the Mishings after their contact with Hinduism ? How did they try to adjust their traditional belief system and forms of worship with growing impact of Hinduism ?

(b) To what extent, they have adopted Assamese language in the place of their own dialect ?

(c) What changes have occurred in their dress, housing pattern, tools and implements due to the impact of the regional culture ?

II

The process of religious contact made the Mishings a part of the regional culture and of the great tradition of Hinduism. Before their advent in the plains, the Mishings were animists. Even today, the traditional pattern of worship is not fully abandoned among them.

In the villages under study, the Mishings practise traditional patterns of worship even though they are Hindus. It has been mentioned earlier that their main deities are the Sun and the Moon (*Donyee-Po:lo*) and they recite the name of these deities in every *Puja* and festival. In this context, it can be mentioned that the Vaishnava *Gosains* (clergy and preachers) and *Satras* (monasteries) are responsible for their conversion to Hinduism (Goswami : 1972). Of course, except the tribal rituals, customs and institutions, the Mishings are similar to the non-tribal Assamese which was reflected even in early writings (see Michell, 1883 : 239). Now-a-days, a considerable number of the Mishings have been converted into *Bhagavatia* or *Mahapuruhia* (based on the doctrines of Shri Sankardev) sects of Hinduism. The process of transformation from the trivial forms of worship to Hinduism is an interesting phenomenon among the Mishings. Hinduism has introduced new priests (Gosain, Bhakats, Hattulas, Satradhikar), new institutions (Namghar, Satra), new mythologies, a new value-system, pattern of stratification (caste) and the notion of purity and pollution through restrictions on food and drinks.

In the place of primitive religion, now-a-days, the religion of the Mishings is popularly known as *Kewalia, Kalsanghati* or *Nisamalia*. These sects are the popular folk level practices of Hinduism. Through these sects also, the Mishings have aligned themselves with the non-tribal regional peasant culture. These folk level religious beliefs and practices have helped them in adjusting their tribal practices with the local Hindu-beliefs and practices.

The adoption of Hinduism led to the emergence of a new group of priests and clergy known as the *Bhakatas* and the *Hattulas*. Formerly, the *Mibu* or the *Miri*, the primitive Mishing priest, was the main person to look after all *Pujas* and festivals. Now-a-days the *Bhakats* and the *Hattulas*, though not necessarily the Brahmins, have been playing the role of preachers, priests and clergy. The introduction of Hindu priests has adversely affected the position of traditional tribal priests known as *Mibu* or *Miri*.

The Vaishnavism in Assam centres around *Namghar* (the place of worship in every village) and *Satras* (monasteries). Now, in Mishing villages, there are *Namghars* and the Mishing villagers belong to the different *Satras*. There are more than two hundred *Satras* in Assam. Through this process also the Mishings are now the part of regional culture. Now they are the part of an institutionalised religious order.

At the popular level, different sects of Hinduism have emerged in Assamese villages in general and the tribal communities in particular. They may be divided into *Nisamalia* or *Kewal Dharma* (worshipper of Goddess or *Shakti*) and *Bhagawatia* (followers of the principles of Shrimad Bhagawat) as propounded by Sankardev.

The *Nisamalia* sect (a mixture of tribal rituals and Hinduism) is known also as *Ratikhowa Dharma, Guput Dharma* and *Amaya Bhakati*. The contact with the *Gosains* (priests) of the *Satras* (monasteries) of Assam is the main reason for the growth of this sect among the Mishings.

The *Sadhu Bura* or the *Bhakats* are now the head of all religious activities of the Mishings. They are ordained into *Bhakats* by the *Gosains* of *Satras* after proper ritual performance. The position of *Kencha Bhakat* (raw or unripe), is slightly lower than *Poka Bhakat* (ripe disciple). With the advent of *Namghar* in Mishing villages, the *Murong* (dormitory) has gradually lost its importance. On the one hand, contacts with Hinduism have led to the emergence of new religious institutions and functionaries. On the other hand, it has helped in the growth of new religious organisations also. The followers of *Bhagawatia* sect have formed *Shankar Sangha* which has been playing an important role in the propagation of Vaishnavism. It has encouraged social service in some selected pockets.

Now, let us try to explain what new religious institutions have been added to the villages under study. In Mohmora and Duhutimukh, all families belong to the *Nisamalia* sect, whereas, in village Barpamua except 20 families, all others are followers of *Nisamalia* sect. In Mishing villages, both sects are having their separate *Namghars*. In all the three villages, there are *Namghars* of *Nisamalia* but *Bhagawatias* are having their *Namghar* near village Barpamua. Both sects have preserved their contacts with *Murong* (dormitory), *Kebang* (tribal council) and the tribal festivals.

If we take the help of a few case studies, we shall be able to explain the nature of Vaishnavism, and its adoptive-mechanism with tribal rituals and customs.

Case Study 5.1

Shri Ingreswar Pegu (age 45 years) of Barpamua village is one of the pioneers in adopting Vaishnavism in Jengraimukh area. According to him, it is difficult to convert the Mishings into *Bhagawatia* as they are incapable of leaving their traditional customs. Those who are converted do not strictly follow the rule of Vaishnavism. He himself participates in tribal rituals, though he is an ardent follower of Vaishnavism. The main aim behind his conversion into Vaishnavism is to reform the religious practices of his community. But, he fails in his attempt. For the sake of the satisfaction of his co-villagers, he participates in traditional rituals also. Like Shri Pegu, the other newly converted disciples are doing the same thing. As a matter of fact, *Bhagawatia* sect is trying to synthesise the animistic form of religious activities of the Mishings with Hinduism. This has created a situation of marginality also.

Case Study 5.2

> Shri Kanai Doley (age 48 years) belongs to *Nisamalia* sect. He was Secretary of the Mishing Kristi Sangha during 1956-58, and was President in 1959. As a result of contact with the *Gosains,* several villagers along with him accepted *Nisamalia* sect. But still, they have not discarded their primitive religious practices. Therefore, lots of traditional rituals are performed by his fellow community members. The performance of tribal rituals requires a lot of wastage. Shri Doley has been trying to make people conscious on this point. And he asks villagers to perform only those rituals which are less harmful to their economy. The followers of *Nisamalia* sect have tried to find out the common elements between tribal forms of worship and Hinduism as practised at the folk level in Assam.

It is worthmentioning that in certain cases the people are conscious about their traditional institutions and sometimes revivalistic trends are also visible. For instance, in my first visit to Mohmora, there was a *Namghar* in the village but there was no *Murong*. I asked the villagers whether they are interested in traditional institutions or not. After one year, when I revisited the village, I found a newly constructed *Murong*. In spite of so much changes in their religious practices, the majority of the Mishings are still the followers of traditional pattern of tribal worship which can be called the hybrid of Hinduism and tribal ritualism. In this context, writings of Hunter (1879:343) will be relevant to quote.

> The Miris (Mishings) in the plains have generally abandoned the vague religious notions of their ancestors, and adopted ideas put into their heads by Assamese Gosains or Brahminical priest, that each of them chose to adopt as their Guru or Spiritual instructor; but all efforts on the part of the Hindus to wean them from their impure mode of living have utterly failed.

The above stated situation still prevails in the villages under study. As regards the religious institutions, the *Namghars* and the *Satras* have been playing important roles in their day to day life.

Now, let us try to derive conclusions on the basis of the analysis of the primary data. Table 5.1 indicates the nature of their visits to the place of worship.

Table 5.1

Visits to Namghar and Satras

Worship place	Frequency of visiting worship-place			Don't visit	Total
	Regularly	Frequently	Occasionally		
Namghar (Village Temples)	16 4.77	67 20.00	226 67.47	26 7.76	335 100.00
Satra (Monastery	—	10 2.98	65 19.62	260 77.62	335 100.00

The regularity is rare in visiting the places of worship and since only 16 (4.77%) respondents regularly visited the *Namghar*. The majority of the respondents (67.47%) visited *Namghar* occasionally. It is because they use to visit *Namghar* only when some rituals are performed. 26 (7.76%) respondents do not visit the worshipping place, whereas, 67 (20.00%) visit frequently. Those who visit the *Namghar* regularly are the *Bhakats* - the Mishing Hinduised priests. The respondents do not visit the *Satras* regularly. The *Satras* of Majuli and other areas of Sibsagar district are visited by the *Bhakats* and few other interested respondents either frequently or occasionally. Out of 335 respondents, 260 (77.62%) have never visited the *Satras*, whereas, 10 (2.98%) visited frequently and 65 (19.40%) occasionally.

The frequency of visiting the place of worship *(Namghar)* is more or less the same irrespective of literacy and illiteracy. Table 5.2 shows the frequency of visits to the *Namghar* according to the level of education.

Table 5.2

Education and Frequency of Visiting Namghar

Education	Frequency of visits			Don't visit	Row total
	Regularly	Frequently	Occasionally		
Illiterate	6 4.61 37.50	14 10.76 20.89	96 73.87 42.47	14 10.76 53.85	130 100.00
Literate	10 6.17 62.50	40 24.69 59.71	107 66.06 47.36	5 3.08 19.23	162 100.00
Undermatric	—	8 24.24 11.94	18 54.55 7.96	7 21.21 26.92	33 100.00
Matriculate	—	5 50.00 7.46	5 50.00 2.21	—	10 100.00
Column Total	16 100.00	67 100.00	226 100.00	26 100.00	335 100.00

As indicated in the above table, out of 16 respondents who visit *Namghar* regularly, 6 (37.50%) are illiterate and 10 (62.50%) are literate. Out of 67 respondents, 14 (20.89%) are illiterate, 40 (59.71%) are literate, 8 (11.94%) are undermatric and 5 (7.46%) are matriculates and above who visit *Namghar* frequently. Again, out of 226 respondents, 96 (42.47%) illiterate, 107 (47.36%) literate, 18 (7.96%) under-matric and 5 (2.21%) matriculates and above visit occasionally. Only 14 (10.76%), out of 130 respondents, do not visit *Namghar*. Contrary to it, *Namghar* is much popular among the literates, because out of 162, only 5 (3.08%) respondents do not visit the place of worship. Anyway, from the above analysis, it is seen that irrespective of literacy and illiteracy the people participate in occasional rituals performed in the *Namghar*.

The transitional stage of the religion and religious activities of the Mishings is fascinating. They have not yet been able to determine whether they should accept a religion which is completely Hindu oriented or not. For instance, in Barpamua village, the villagers informed that about 15-20 families were converted into *Bhagawatia* or Vaishnavism in 1961. The converted families avoided all tribal practices for a few years which were performed earlier. But this habit did not last long. Most of the families left Vaishnavism and again started to practise their traditional rituals. In Jengraimukh Tinali, the *Bhagawatias* of the area constructed a *Namghar* in 1961, specially for the newly converted families. The families who are still performing the rules of the newly converted cult, have been performing religious duties daily.

Food Habit

The food habits of the Mishings, as found in the field, are now-a-days similar with the non-tribal neighbouring Hindus. But, to a certain extent, their food habits still have a similarity with the Adis of Arunachal (Elwin, 1957: 77-80; Roy, 1966: 33-36). Before the acceptance of Hinduism and the impact of non-tribal Hindus to a greater extent, the Mishings ate pig, fowl, beef, and drank spirit and beer, and had no caste notion about the preparation of food (Hunter, 1979: 343). Now, after Hinduisation, lot of changes are taking place in their food habits. As found in the field, rice (*apin*) is the staple food of the villagers. The people have three meals in a day. One is taken in morning, one in mid-day and another in the evening. Though, the villagers now-a-days know various processes of cooking, yet boiled food is still popular among them. Along with rice, boiled edible leaves (e.g. *dermi, ombe, pakkam, takuk* etc.), meat (*adin*) and fish (*ango*) are some of the popular food items of the villagers. Dried meat and fish are very popular.

In comparison to other food items made of rice, *apong* (rice beer) is a much popular drink among the villagers. It is of two types, viz. *Nagin apong* and *po:ro apong*. Out of these two types, any one is always taken at the time of meal. Moreover, at first the villagers offer *apong* to their guests which is regarded as honour shown to the guests. *Apong*, *adin* (meat), *ango* (fish) edible leaves are also used as a part of food items in their festivals and ritual ceremonies.

The impact of Hinduism and regional culture is found in the changing pattern of food habit of the Mishings. The Hinduisation has taught them the notion of purity and pollution. And for that the *Gosains* of the *Satras* have played the major role, because they taught the people about what should be taken and what should not be taken. As informed by the villagers, formerly, beef was the inevitable part of their food item, but after the influence of the *Gosains*, beef eating is prohibited among them. The following changes in food, drink habits and entertainment are visible in the villages :

(1) The villagers, now-a-days, offer betelnut (*tamul-pan*) to the guests in place of *apong*. The betelnut is a part of the regional Assamese culture which is accepted by the Mishings.

(2) Now-a-days, eggs (*api*), milk (*gakir*), oil (*tulang*) are included in their food items which did not form the part of their food habit in the past.

(3) It is seen that most of the villagers have acquaintance with tea. As a drink, tea is popular among them only next to *apong*.

(4) Most of the traditional food items (pig, beef etc.) have been abandoned by the villagers after their conversion to Vaishnavism.

Apart from the influence of Hinduism, the growth of marketing centres and improvement in transportation have been playing important role in changing food habits of the Mishings. The villagers of Mohmora are now used to visit hotels and tea stalls at Jonai. Similarly, the villagers of Duhutimukh (near Dhemaji) and Barpamua (near Jengraimukh Tinali) frequently visit hotels and tea stalls. The villagers informed that since their childhood they had the continuous contact with the non-tribal Assamese.

Case Study 5.3

Shri Mohan Sarah (age–45 years) of Mohmora village says that his co-villagers migrated from different places to his village. The villagers have a close and continuous contact with the non-tribal Assamese. Regarding changes in their life, he says, "Formerly we did not use oil to prepare curry, but now-a-days it is difficult to do without it. Even *tamul-pan* and tea are part of our daily food items. The *apong* as the part of tribal culture is still popular, but the *tamul-pan*, no doubt, is the gift of the Assamese culture."

Case Study 5.4

According to Shri Bhudeswar Pegu (age–45 years) of Barpamua village in Majuli, "not only to speak of food habits, cultural change is essential for the development of the Mishing society. It is true that we are changing day by day. But it does not mean that we have completely avoided our traditional food practices in *pujas* and rituals." He is in favour of total cultural change for the development of his community.

Language

The Mishing language belongs to the northern branch of the Indo-Tibeto-Burman languages (Padun, 1972:340). There is such similarity of their language with the languages of Adis and Nishis of Arunachal Pradesh. All the three tribes call their languages with the name of their own tribe, i.e. *Nishi-agom, Adi-agom* and *Mishing-agom.* Usually, they call the language as *tani-agom* (human speech or language). The similarity is visible because the Mishings were once a tribe of Arunachal Pradesh.

Though there is a common language among the Mishings, different tone in each sub-group is often visible. Each of the sub-groups viz., *Chayengia, Pagro, Delu, Ayengia, Dambukial, Samua* have slightly separate tones of their own which are different from one another. *Ayengia, Pagro, Delu* sub-groups have much similarity within themselves, whereas, *Samua* and *Moying* have similarity. But as the language is basically the same, all the people can follow and understand each other easily.

It was found in the field that the process of acculturation in the case of adoption of Assamese language was also visible among the Mishings. Assamese language is as popular as the language of their own. If we go back to history, it is seen that in the early part of the sixteenth century, the Mishings came into contact with the Ahom (Devi, 1968), and most probably, they knew Assamese since the Ahom reign in Assam. In the later period, *Gosains* and Brahmins advocated the Philosophy of Hinduism and Vaishnavism to the Mishings through Assamese language. Moreover, as mentioned earlier, the Mishings have the opportunity to maintain close and continuous contact with the non-tribal Assamese. Naturally, the impact of Assamese language is inevitable among them. They have adopted various Assamese words in the Mishing language. In short, Assamese language became the part and parcel in the daily conversation of the respondents. Moreover, majority of the respondents know Bengali and Hindi. Their common language next to Assamese is Hindi. English is known to the educated respondents only. The sources by which the respondents know three languages are numerous. The following table shows few of the sources of their knowing these languages.

Table 5.3

Sources of Knowing Different Languages by the Respondents

Languages	Sources of learning different languages						
	Students	Leaders	Schools	Marketing centre	Traders	No opinion	Total
Assamese	—	—	204 60.91	70 20.89	61 18.20	—	335 100.00
Bengali	—	—	46 13.74	98 29.25	98 29.25	93 27.76	335 100.00
Hindi	—	—	73 12.79	130 38.81	115 34.33	17 5.07	335 100.00
English	6 1.79	—	113 39.70	—	—	196 58.51	335 100.00
Any other (Nepali)	—	—	—	44 13.13	44 13.13	247 73.74	335 100.00

The table given above shows that the schools, marketing centres and traders have been playing significant roles for knowing other languages. Both marketing centres and traders are well known as catalysts of cultural exchange. Out of 335 respondents, 70 (20.89%) and 61 (18.20%) know Assamese language through marketing centres and traders respectively. Other 204 (60.91%) respondents have learnt it through schools. In case of the Bengali language, 98 (29.25%) of them learnt this language through marketing centres and equal number of respondents picked it up through traders. Both marketing centres and traders have been playing very significant roles in spreading Hindi language among the respondents. 130 (38.81%) and 115 (34.33%) respondents learnt Hindi through marketing centres and traders respectively. In case of Nepali language also, the same sources of learning the languages have played significant roles. It is worthmentioning that the respondents have not chosen leaders as the sources of knowing other languages. English is known only to the educated respondents. 113 (39.70%) out of 335 respondents learnt English through schools whereas 6 (1.79%) respondents picked up English through students. The table shows that next to Assamese, the most well-known language of the respondents is Hindi.

In some areas, especially in Lakhimpur sub-division of Lakhimpur district and Golaghat sub-division of Sibsagar district, the acculturation in the field of language is so deep that in several Mishing villages, the people have almost forgotten the Mishing language. Among the non-Mishing speaking Mishings, there are five divisions, viz., *Temar, Samuguria, Bongkual, Bihia* and *Bebejia* (Loying, 1972 : 28). The Mishings of these divisions have completely forgotten the Mishing language. At present, their main language is Assamese. Only few Mishing words and kinship terms are used by them in daily conversation. It is not sure whether the non-Mishing people formed these sub-groups during the Ahom-Chutia conflict and *Mon* (Burmese) aggression or the Mishings accepted the Assamese language in place of their own. These sub-groups and families are not found in the villages of the present study.

The major observations on language can be summarised as follows:

(1) All the respondents, irrespective of the levels of literacy, can speak and understand Assamese language. Next to the Mishing dialect, Assamese is the predominant medium for communication with other people.

(2) In conversations, use of Assamese words and sentences are common among the respondents. It is found in few educated families that the young children do not know their own language. It is noteworthy that the parents of such families are proud of their children as their sons and daughters can speak sound and fluent Assamese.

(3) Next to Assamese, Hindi is the most popular language of the respondents.

(4) Most of the respondents are of the view that in future, Mishing language may be replaced by Assamese language, if proper written and printed literature in Mishing language is not developed. The respondents told that like the *Samugurias* (as discussed earlier) they might forget their dialect if the acceptance of Assamese language continues as it is continuing today.

(5) All the *mantras* for ritual activities used by the *Bhakats* and *Hattulas* are in Assamese language. These *mantras* are the abstract from *Kirtana, Namghusa* and *Bhagavat Gita.* These are the influences of Sankardev's Vaishnavism through the *Gosains* of the *Satras.* Thus religion has helped in the spread of Assamese language.

The respondents are in favour of the gradual change in all spheres of the Mishing culture.

Case Study 5.5

Shri Babulal Paw, 54, of Mohmora village is a successful contractor. His economic condition is sound. He told that as a contractor he had to know almost all the languages of his locality. He feels "Assamese language is a must for us. So is the case with Hindi. Our own dialect is not fully developed, therefore we have no other alternative but to accept other languages." More or less the same views were expressed by other respondents also.

Case Study 5.6

Shri Bodiram Mili, aged 70, one of the oldest villagers of Duhutimukh, said in the discussion that all acceptance irrespective of religion and other elements of culture could be tolerated if they were in favour of the development of our society.

Case Study 5.7

By expressing the same view, Shrimati Debeswari Doley, 32 years old widow of Barpamua village told that she was having an interest to educate her children. If it is possible, she will not mind if her children accept other languages or culture instead of her own : "because", she says, "education and economy are more essential than the medium of instruction or language problem".

Pattern of Houses

The Mishing village consists of 10 to 100 or more households built on bamboo platform. The Mishings generally build their houses haphazardly within the village area, and to a certain extent perpendicular to the river flow if the villages are situated on the bank of the river. It has been found in the field that the villagers under study have their houses on piles, where the floor is about 4 ft. to 5 ft. above the ground. The level for the floor is obtained from stilts. It may be made of wood or bamboo. On the stilts they form the floor with the match of thick bamboo splits. The platform ultimately forms the main house which is walled by matting of split bamboo. The complete houses are usually about 40 ft. to 100 ft. in length and 10 ft. to 15 ft. in breadth. The main items for the construction of a house are wood, bamboo and thatch.

As found in the field, a house is not divided into different rooms. There are only two doors (*yabgo*) in the house, one in front (*tupak yabgo*) and the other in the back (*yapkur yabgo*). Windows are not found. One *varandah* is constructed in the front (*Tungeng*) where there is a ladder (*ko:bang*) leading from the *tungeng* to the ground and another varandah is in the back (*yapkur tungeng*). The villagers keep their mortar (*ki:par*) and loom (*tarte*) in *tu:pok* which is in the ground and in front of the *tungeng*. The fire place (*meram*) situated in the middle of the house is noticeable. Several *merams* are found in a house which depend upon the size of the household. The fire place is constructed by fixing wooden trays in gaps covering them with earth. Over the hearth hangs a three-tired (sometimes more) bamboo shelf, which is used to dry fuel, meat, fish and other items. In the upper side of the house, parallel to the *meram*, the head of the family sits and the lower side is generally occupied by the females. The fire place is important because it makes the division of the whole house. The upper side of the *meram* is called *rising* and the lower side is *koktok*. They sleep in the upper side (*so:yer* or *pe:jong*) of the house.

Acculturation is visible in regard to the housing pattern of the respondents. The respondents whose economic condition is sound, constructed Assam type pucca building in place of their traditional houses. The people are not in favour of inhygienic, traditional houses. Whenever the money is available, they try to construct either pucca building or house of wooden platform and few of them choose *kachcha matti ghar*. But unfortunately, in each of the pucca buildings as found in the field, the owners constructed one typical Mishing house, which according to them, is essential for cooking, *pujas* and festivals. It is observed that the two main reasons behind the construction of pucca building are the sound economy and education. The following table indicate the same.

Table 5.4

Causes and Preferences given by the Respondents for the Construction of Modern Type of Houses

Causes	Preference			No preference	Total
	First	Second	Third		
Education	12 3.58	23 6.86	6 1.78	294 87.78	335 100.00
Sound economic condition	26 7.76	7 2.08	8 2.38	294 87.78	335 100.00
Influence of non-tribal Assamese	7 2.08	6 1.79	28 8.35	294 87.78	335 100.00

As seen in the table, out of 335 respondents, 12 (3.58%) have given first preference to education for the construction of modern type of houses, and 23 (6.86%) the second, 6 (2.78%) respondents have given it the third preference. 26 (7.76%) respondents have given first preference to sound economic condition as the main cause of construction of modern type of houses. 7 (2.08%) have emphasised on the influence of non-tribal Assamese as the first preference. The table shows that the people generally have given stress on the sound economic condition and education for the well-to-do life which will ultimately lead to their social change.

So far as the pucca buildings in the villages are concerned, 16 Assam type pucca buildings are found in the three villages under study. The first building was constructed in 1958 in Barpamua village. From this it can be assumed that construction of modern houses started in the Mishing villages around the mid fifties. Now-a-days, in place of traditional houses, *Kachcha matti* houses are also seen. It is found under this study that such houses were constructed first in the year 1969. However, in each of the three villages, traditional houses are still predominantly higher than the modern hygienic pucca buildings.

Some of the major changes as observed in the field are as follows :

(1) Most of the villagers like to have modern houses in place of their traditional housing pattern. Those who are in a position to construct new concrete buildings, they never like traditional unhygienic houses. The respondents who are not economically sound they tried to construct houses with wooden platforms.

(2) The villagers who are having *matti ghar* like the surrounding non-tribal Assamese are of the opinion that *matti ghar* houses

of bamboo are much more comfortable than the *chung ghar*. According to them *chung ghar* (house on platform) is essential only in such places where flood is a constant phenomenon.

(3) It is 'however' observed that the guardians generally construct small *matti ghars* for their grown up children who are studying in schools and colleges. They told that *chung ghar* was not at all convenient place for the purpose of study of their children, therefore, if possible, they are in favour of the construction of pucca building. They never mind if it leads to changing their traditional pattern.

(4) One of the most striking features, as observed in the field is that, though the economically sound families have constructed pucca buildings but in each building, there is a traditional *chung ghar* which is used either by aged persons or for *pujas* and festivals. The aged villagers are incapable of adjusting themselves with modern pucca building and prefer traditional *chung ghar*.

(5) It is seen that most of the villagers have their *Pak ghar* (kitchen hall) which is attached to the main house. This is one of the most significant influence of the non-tribal Assamese. Because, formerly the Mishings had no separate kitchen. It used to be within the sleeping halls of their houses.

(6) Another significant change observed in the field is that some of the villagers have guest rooms in their houses. This is one of the direct influence of the non-tribal Assamese. As a member of the same community, the investigator has the experience that few years back most of the Mishing villagers had no such separate drawing rooms for the guests. The guests or the co-villagers have to enter directly to the fire place for any sort of discussion. But now-a-days, a separate room, which is used as drawing room (guest room) is often seen in the households.

Dress

The dress of the Mishings can be divided into two distinct types as indicated by Roy (1966:74) in case of the tribes of Arunachal. The two distinct types are (i) general dress for everyday use, and (ii) special dress for festivals and ceremonial functions. As observed in the field, the dress for the everyday use of the people is very simple. The dress of the men is similar to non-tribal Assamese. A simple white dhoti (*ugon*) or sometimes a long coloured *dumer* (towel) and a shirt (*galuk*) is the dress of the men. The dress of the women is also simple, but divided into two pieces of garments. They generally wear a skirt (*mosanam* age) covering the part from the waist to the knee. The upper piece (*gasong* or *gero*) fastened above the breast falling along with the skirt. Occasionally, a blouse is seen to cover the upper part of the body.

The dress for particular occasions is the special product of their loom. In these dresses, they use the mixture of various colours, e.g. red, black, green, yellow are common. On special occasions, a man wears a skirt (*mibu galuk*) over his usual dress and a *dumer* (towel) is a must. Only few of them use *Paguri* (turban). The dresses on special occasions are used in such a way, so that, a man will look like *gam* or leader. The dress of the women is same as they use daily, but the dresses for festivals and functions are more coloured and decorated. The plain dresses without colour and decoration are generally not used in festivals and rituals. Women are fond of various types of ornaments. Ear and neck ornaments (*kentumaduli*), chains (*tadok*), different type of bracelets (*konge*) are very much common among the women.

All the dresses, especially of the women, are the products of loom. The Mishing women are famous for weaving in Assam. Few of their products, viz., *gadu gasar, tapum gasar, dumer, mibu galuk, shekreg, neshag ri:bi* are worth mentioning. The women use two types of looms. First is used like the Adis of Arunachal, one end fastened in a parallel bar (*tututa*) and the other end fastened in the waist. This type of loom can easily be used wherever they like in the cultivating field, inside the house as it is small and can be handled easily. Some of the products of this type of loom are *gadu, mibu galuk* and *sogon*. The other type is like the loom used by the non-tribal Assamese. Yarn for the loom is generally brought from the market. But the Mishing women, as found in the field, grow at least a little amount of cotton for their loom. This is done especially for *gadu*, which is a prestigious product, and which is offered as gift by a mother to her newly married son. Ginning and spinning is still done by the women themselves. The most striking feature of the Mishing women is that their weaving products are with pattern and colour of perfect taste.

What is observed in the three villages under study is that in spite of so much of excellent weaving productions, the machine made cloth is much popular among the villagers. Almost all the villagers, irrespective of male and female, wear machine-made clothes. No doubt weaving is still popular among them, but its place is being gradually taken over by the machine-made productions. The following table has given an idea of the prevalence of weaving and attitude towards mill-made clothes of the respondents:

Table 5.5

Domestic Weaving and Attitude towards Mill-made Clothes

Prevalence of weaving	Attitude towards mill-made cloth			Row Total
	Like	Dislike	Neutral	
Prevalent	248 77.99 100.00	—	70 22.01 85.37	318 100.00
Not prevalent		5 29.41 100.00	12 70.59 14.63	17 100.00
Column Total	248 100.00	5 100.00	82 100.00	335 100.00

The table indicates that out of 318 respondents, in whose family weaving is prevalent, 248 (77.99%) respondents like mill-made clothes. Attitude of the 70 (22.01%) respondents towards mill-made cloth is neutral. Notably, only in 17 families weaving is not prevalent and out of it 5 (29.41%) respondents dislike machine-made production, 12(70.59%) respondents are of neutral attitude. The result, as found in the table, is that mill-made clothes have deeply been penetrating into the life of the villagers in spite of popularity of weaving productions.

There are various causes responsible for the changing of dress pattern of the respondents. The primary causes, as informed by the villagers, are education, sound economic condition, as found easily in the market and so on. All respondents told that they were accepting mill-made clothes not because they totally disliked weaving productions. According to them, weaving is a time consuming device, and even if they like it, their production cannot cope with the need. Therefore, they are bound to depend upon the clothes available in the market. The following table shows the causes responsible for the changing of dress pattern and preferences given by the respondents.

As seen in the table, 171 (51.06%) respondents have given first preference in education as the main cause for changing-dress pattern of their society. Contrary to it, the lowest respondents 12 (3.58%) have given first preference on unpopularity of weaving. In the second preference, the highest respondents 109 (32.55%) are found in the causes of sound economic condition and neighbouring non-tribal Assamese. Only 9 (2.68%) and 30 (8.96%) respondents preferred the first preference for the influence of neighbouring non-tribal Assamese and market place. 196 (58.52%) respondents have given fourth preference in unpopularity of weaving as one of the causes of change in dresses, which ultimately means the popularity of weaving among the villagers.

Table 5.6

Causes Responsible for Changing Dress-Pattern and Preference Given by the Respondents

Causes	Preference					
	1st	2nd	3rd	4th	5th	Total
Education	171 51.06	71 21.19	74 22.08	19 5.67	—	335 100.00
Sound economic condition	73 21.79	109 32.55	103 30.74	50 14.92	—	335 100.00
Unpopularity of weaving	12 3.58	43 12.84	84 25.07	196 58.07	—	335 100.00
Neighbour-ing non-tribal Assamess	79 .23.58	109 32.55	72 21.49	66 19.70	9 2.68	335 100.00
Any other (as found easily in market)	93 27.76	94 28.05	107 31.05	11 3.28	30 8.96	335 100.00

The findings based on observation can be summarised as follows :

(1) The dresses of the men are similar to those of the neighbouring non-tribal Assamese, but the dresses of the women are still dissimilar with those of the non-tribal women. But the educated Mishing women are using the same dresses as the Assamese women.

(2) Except in *pujas* and festivals, the villagers do not use traditional dresses. The traditional dresses are preserved like their property and whenever needed are worn with care.

(3) Weaving is still popular among the villagers. Traditional dresses are the product of their weaving. Though yarn for weaving is usually bought from the market, the women still grow cotton for few of their special productions in weaving.

(4) Few of the weaving productions, *tapum gasor, gadu, dumer, mibu galuk* etc. are sold by the women to meet the other daily needs.

(5) Now-a-days, the clothes which are available in market are the most common dresses irrespective of male and female.

Tools and Implements

The villagers under study are essentially agriculturists. Therefore, all the implements of the villagers are agriculture oriented. It was observed in the field that only a few agricultural implements were used by the villagers. It was seen that all the agricultural implements were the direct influence of the non-tribal Assamese. As the Mishings were *Jhum* cultivators during the time of their habitation in the hills of Arunachal, they had only few agricultural tools. They were *egin* (bamboo baskets), *epo, eging, kuyap* (axes), *dao* or *yoktung* etc. After the migration to the plains of Assam, they accepted the method of wet cultivation and started to adopt the non-tribal Assamese way of cultivation. *Nangal-juwali* (plough), *dila, moi, kashi* etc., according to the aged villagers, are the gift of the Assamese culture to the Mishings.

The people of the three villages possess cage-like baskets for pigs and fowls. They have separate type of cage-like baskets for each stage of pigs and fowls, viz. *yegum, yegshup, yegpur-porog pekang, porog pera, porog peter*. Their acquisitions from non-tribal Assamese are cowshed, buffaloshed, and numerous other domestic possessions. Few major tools for fishing, while the Mishings were in the hills of Arunachal, were *e:opuk* (bow and arrow) and few other arrow-type (*jamborok*) sharp-pointed tools. Trap-like *porang, dingarang, jurki, jakoi* etc. and varieties of nets (*eshap*), according to the villagers, are not their traditional possessions. These tools are the direct gift of the plains people of Assam.

As observed in the field, almost all the household utensils of the villagers are similar to those of the non-tribal Assamese. Now-a-days, it is rather difficult to find out the utensils which are of Mishing origin. Utensils like earthenware (*ki:ling*), *aram-bati* (metallic dishes) are not of their own origin and for these utensils they depend either on local potters or on the local market. The modern furniture like tables, chairs and utensils like cup, glass etc. are found in almost all households of the respondents under study. The modern tools and implements, now-a-days, are part and parcel of their life.

It is, however, accepted by all the respondents that changes in all aspects of life is a phenomenon which cannot be resisted.

Case Study 5.8

Shri Mohen Sarah (age — 45 years) of Mohmora, told that acculturation in respect of these aspects was a must due to the time factor. The adjustment with the time and situation was vital, and in doing so traditional dresses have been replaced by modern dresses and so also in other cases.

Case Study 5.9

Both as a cultivator and Govt. employee Shri Lakheswar Kardong, aged 40 years of Duhutimukh, is of the opinion that the pattern of their households should be changed as their traditional houses are unhygienic. He said, "I am in favour of modern pucca building because of its durability and hygienity. Our dresses are compelled to be of machine-made even though we like weaving productions, because the latter is not capable of producing according to the needs."

Case Study 5.10

Another respondent, Shri Lengkeng Pegu (age — 58 years) of Barpamua village, informed that during the time of his youth, the elder villagers used to wear a simple *dhoti* and a shirt. Such dresses were regarded traditional dress during that time though the clothes were purchased from market. But now-a-days, modern dresses with modern designs have become prevalent in their society. According to him, "As our society is changing in all aspects, it is natural that house pattern, dresses, tools and implements of our society will be changed accordingly."

III

It is seen in the chapter that acculturation has taken place in all aspects of cultural life of the Mishing society. It has been found that acculturation is continuing among the villagers not necessarily because of acceptance of non-tribal elements. Various other factors responsible for acculturation are summarised as follows :

(1) One of the main factors for the acceptance of the implements of non-tribal Assamese culture is the ecology. Since the migration from the hills of Arunachal Pradesh in the 13th century, the Mishings have been living with the non-tribals in the plains of Assam. Therefore, there have been close and continuous contacts with the neighbouring non-tribal villagers. It ultimately led to the cultural change of the Mishings.

(2) Due to the close and continuous contact, the first change faced by the Mishings was in their religious practices. They were converted into Hinduism by the *Brahmins* and *Gosains* of the *Satras*. It ultimately paved the way for the abolition of some of the traditional beliefs and practices. Present-day religious cult of the Mishings, which is known as *Kalhanghati* or *Nisamalia* and the priest like the *Bhakats* and the *Hattulas* are the product of the acceptance of Hinduism through *Gosains*. In this context, the impact of the neighbouring Hindu villagers of various communities is also noteworthy. The Mishings derived the influence of Hinduism from these villagers.

(3) After the acceptance of Hinduism, naturally, all the primitive habits of the Mishings have a tremendous change. From the very early stage, the trend of change is gradual. Due to the influence of Hinduism, they gave up the habit of beef and buffalo eating. The meat of Mithun, one of the famous animals of Arunachal, according to the aged villagers, was very popular among them. Now-a-days, the Mishings have left that habit. The use of oil and other delicacies are the gift of the non-tribals to the Mishings. That can be proved till today, because instead of frying, boiled meat, fish and leafy vegetables are still popular among them.

(4) In conclusion, it can be said that change is a vital phenomenon among the Mishings. At the present moment, acculturation is continuing in all aspects of their life. And if the process continues due to increase of educated Mishings, development in economy and in other aspects, the ultimate result may be the detribalisation of the Mishings. Till today, no measures are found to be taken for the preservation of tribal practices and customs among them.

References

1 See N. Padun's (1971:231) *Mishing Boyan Silpa*, and T.C. Pamegam's (1972:237) *Boyan Silpat Mishing Jiyari* for the elaborate idea of the Mishing fabrics. Essays in B. Kagyung (ed.), *Mishing Sanskritir Alekhya*, 1972, Birubari, Guwahati.

Borua, B.K.
1951 A Cultural History of Assam (early period). Lawyer's Book Stall, Guwahati, Assam.

Chaterji, S.K.
1951 Kirata Jana Krit - The Indo-Mongoloids : their contribution to the history and culture of India. Based upon Pratibha Devi Lectures, delivered at Jorhat, Assam, in 1947, published in 1951 by the Asiatic Society, 1 Park Street, Calcutta-16.

Dubey, S.M.
1978 Transformation of Tribal Communities in North-East India. Cyclostyled, working paper, Panel II, The All India Sociological Conference, Jabalpur, December 28-30, 1978.

Elwin, Verrier
1964 A Philosophy for NEFA, Shillong.

Gait, Sir Edward
1905 A History of Assam. Thacker Spink & Co. (1933) P. Ltd., Calcutta.

Goswami, B.B.
1972 The Tribes of Assam : Few Comments on their social and cultural ties with the non-tribes. In K. Suresh Singh (ed.), Tribal situation in India (Proceedings of a seminar), India Institute of Advance Studies, Simla.

Hunter, W.W.
1879 A Statistical Account of Assam. Vol. II, Trubner & Co., London. Reprinted 1975 by B.R. Publishing Corporation, Delhi.

Herskovitz, M.J.
1938 Acculturation : The study of culture contact. New York : J.J. Augustin.

Loying, T.
1972 *Mishing Bhasa Nukua Mishing*. In B. Kagyung (ed.), *Mishing Sanskritir Alekhya*, 1972, Birubari, Guwahati.

Mead, Margaret
1932 The changing culture of an Indian tribe. New York : Columbia University Press.

Michell, John F.
1833 The North-East Frontier of India (A topographical, political and military report). Reprinted 1973 by Vivek Publishing House, Delhi.

Majumder, D.N.
1949 The Changing Canvas of Tribal Life. Eastern Anthropologist I, Vol. III.
1972 Acculturation among the Hajong of Meghalaya. Man in India 1, Vol. 52, January-March.

Mipun, J.

1976 Acculturation, Communication and Development among the Dimasa Kacharis of the North Cachar Hills district in Assam. The North-Eastern Research Bulletin, Vol. VII, Summer.

Padun, N.

1972 *Mishing Bhasa*. In B. Kagyung (ed.) ibid.

Redfield, Robert

1955 The Social Organization of Tradition. Far Eastern Quarterly, Vol. 15, pp. 13-21.

Roy, Sachin

1966 Aspects of Padam Minyong Culture. N.E.F.A., Shillong.

Sengupta, S.K.

1966 Assimilation of Cultural Traits by the Mahlis of Midnapur, Calcutta: Calcutta University.

Srivastava, S.K.

1949 Some Problems of Culture Contacts among the Tharus. Eastern Anthropologist I, Vol. III.

Vidyarthi, L.P. and B.K. Rai

1976 The Tribe Culture of India. The Concept Publishing Co., Delhi.

CHAPTER VI

IMPACT OF MODERN COMMUNICATION

I

The early ethnographers like Hutton (1921), Gorer (1938), Furer-Haimendorf (1930) and others treated the tribes as isolates. It was rather a fact during the time of their studies on the tribes. But a careful analysis of these ethnographic studies does show that even at that time the level of interaction between the tribes and the non-tribes was significant. Economic necessities had been the main reason for these interactions where oral communication played the significant role. In this context, the study of Damle (1955) can be referred to where he says that the penetration of modern ideas and knowledge in Indian villages are the result of improvement of the communication system in India. While discussing the trade and barter of the Akas, Sinha (1962 : 48-52) writes :

> The trade of the Akas, as such, is of two kinds : one which they carry on among themselves and what conveniently called the inter-village trade, and secondly, their trade with the plains. The system of barter is more practical in the mutual trade between their own villages and to some extent with the neighbouring Bangi people with whom they come into contact for trade purposes. In their trade with the people in the plains (non-tribes), they have to deal essentially in cash.... with the money they get in return for their commodities, they usually purchase their necessity like cloth, silver ornaments and utensils. Their trade with the plains (non-tribes) has introduced a good deal of currency among them.

It shows that the Akas have been interacting with a wider world which included non-tribes and tribes alike. While discussing the Assamese culture, Das (1967) argues that Assamese culture has adopted ideas, beliefs, and institutions of the surrounding Mongoloid population.

He says that there has been a mutual borrowing between the hill people and those of the valley in Assam. That was possible on account of mutual exchange of goods through barter, linguistic interaction, and interpretation of religious ideas. Majumder (1967) describes the social organization of the Koch of the Garo hills and their gradual merging into Hindu society. Roy Burman and Thukral (1970) have tried to provide a picture of the dynamic process of interaction among the various tribes and non-tribes of North-East India. According to them (1970 : 107) :

> A change is taking place in the perspective of the larger setting for social interactions. It is significant to note that for most of the tribes of this region the etymological meaning of their name is 'man'. It appears that in their traditional world view they divided the mankind into two groups–one consisting of themselves only and other consisting of the rest of humanity. With the expansion of communication, intensification of contact with and being drawn in the orbit of world technological order, the frame of reference to these communities for social interaction is rapidly undergoing change. For various purposes they perceive their reference groups differently depending on their stage of cultural development.

These happenings are the result of communication and interaction among the people—both tribes and non-tribes. As pointed out by Mishra (1973), for these interactions, people must have the communication facilities which ultimately help in accepting modern ideas. And in most of the cases the leaders and the students played as the media of communication who help in the interaction of the people with their reference groups (see Lionberger and Mishra 1976).

Society can be defined as a structure of interconnecting communication networks (Hockings, 1977). Of course, communication is a very general term and it is difficult to define it within a specific framework. Along with the radio and television, Hockings, (1977:475-76) says that different types of communication networks, such as, transportation of people and their materials, mechanical system for transmission of personal messages, media of mass-communication and interpersonal linkages are very essential in the field of the sociology of communication. Keeping in view these points, the following aspects of communication are attempted to study in this chapter :

(1) The phase of oral communication among the Mishings and their linkages with other communities.

(2) Introduction of roads and its impact on the Mishings.
(3) Introduction of railways and its impact.
(4) Impact of the marketing centres.
(5) Impact of post and telegraph, radio listening and newspaper reading.
(6) Interaction and communication with religious, political and educational elite.

II

Before the British rule in India, the Mishings had low rate of interactions with the non-tribes. Though, they were within the plain districts of Assam, the Mishings were dwelling in the isolated places near the river banks of Assam. Due to that, their mode of communication and interaction with the non-tribes was similar with the other tribes of North-East India. Trade was one of the main sources of communication among the Mishings which was also the only source of communication of the other hill tribes. In context of the tribes of Arunachal Pradesh, Roy Burman and Thakral, (1970:93), said :

> The trade between Apatanis and their Dafla and Miri neighbours is largely based on the complementary nature of their economics. The exchange of surplus Apatanis rice against Dafla or Miri animals is, therefore, to the advanage of both sides. Besides, buying mithun and pigs for rice, the Apatanis obtain from Daflas almost all the cotton required for their highly developed weaving industries.

The interaction between the tribes and the non-tribes started gradually when the tribes were converted either to Christianity or to Hinduism. One of the main reasons behind it is the improvement of communication facilities. As a result, alike the other tribes of North-East India, acculturation started among the Mishings of Assam. The non-tribal Hindu population of Assam have gradually been influencing the language and speech pattern of the Mishings. The increasing use of Assamese, Bengali and Hindi by them is indicative of this process. As the communication facilities are increasing, the process of acculturation has also been increasing. The same process has been discussed in this chapter in the light of the points indicated earlier.

In their pre-literate and primitive system, oral communications were more important. The Mishings used a dialect which was akin to Adi group of dialects. Naturally, the range of their communication, even after their migration to the plains, was oriented and confined to the tribes having kinship relationship with them. When they moved to the plains, probably for a long time, they had their compact tribal territory. Gradually, they came in contact with other communities - such as Deories, Chutias, Ahoma. There were three different dimensions of their oral communication :

(a) among themselves and with the tribes of the hills, they used their own dialects ;

(b) to barter and to interact with their neighbouring communities, they had to pick up Assamese language ; and

(c) in the process of interaction, they came within the field of Hinduism and Assamese became more prevalent among them.

In the isolated tribal system, barter, conversion and growing interaction with the neighbours influenced their pattern and range of communication. Since they were settled on the banks of the Brahmaputra, Subansiri and other small rivers, they were linked with their neighbours and other villages by boats. The Mishings were expert boatmen and since time immemorial, they used to construct their boats. In this respect, after migration to the plains, their technique was much developed. They use boats for fishing also. Boats are used to go to the field, to transport the products to the local markets and to participate in festivals and ceremonies.

Traditionally, the Mishings were expert elephant catchers and trainers. Formerly, almost all well-to-do Mishing families used to have elephants. Even today, possession of elephant is a symbol of social prestige.

While they were within the isolated tribal system, sending of intra-village messages were done mostly by individual messengers, by beating drum or by holding *kebang*. The Mishings were having associations within the village. The *kebang* (village council), *Yame-member* (youths) associations had recruited persons for sending messages. Within the village, the messages of the *kebang* were circulated to the villagers by the *Barik* (messenger) either by beating drum or by delivering the news loudly. The date of holding and the decisions of the *kebang* were the usual messages circulated by the *Barik* within the village. For the circulation of the messages of the *Yame-member* association, *Deka Bora* (messenger of the boys) and *Maiki Bora* (messenger of the girls) were appointed. All these recruitments were for a term of one year only. After one year, new recruitments were done. Concessions in all matters within the village were given to them during their term of office as messengers.

The Mishings way of life is reflected in their folk tales and folk songs. These have been going on for generation after generation as messages among the people. The folk tales and songs inform them about their ancestors, their way of life etc. *Oinitom*, the famous folk song of the Mishings, is used as a media of sending personal messages. Among the youths, sending of personal messages through *Oinitom* have been going on since time immemorial. They usually express their love and affection towards their beloved by *Oinitom*. Signs and symbols are also used as a means of informing other people. For instance, at the time of performance of *Dobur puja*, they construct a gate at the main entrance road of the village. The gate is a sign of caution to the outsiders, so that no outsider can enter into the village at the time of *puja*.

As mentioned earlier, the means of inter-village communication were mainly the boats and elephants. In sending messages to other villages, usually the intra-village messengers were entitled to use the same. These included the communication among themselves and also with other communities.

Introduction of Roads and its Impact on the Mishings

It is known from early writings that the district of Lakhimpur was vast and, therefore, the transport communication was in very poor condition (see Robinson, 1841:332; Hunter, 1879:291-92). During the British period, Sadiya, Dibrugarh and North Lakhimpur were the most advanced British centres. But the transport communication was not satisfactory. The British administrators had to suffer a lot in implementing administrative planning. The early picture of the district, from where the two villages Mohmora and Duhutimukh have been selected for study, is given by Hunter (1879 : 292) as follows :

> The first tract now forms the sub-division of North Lakhimpur and consists of a long narrow plain gradually sloping southwards from the hills to the banks of the Brahmaputra and Luhit rivers. This division is said to have suffered more from the calamities which the later events in the history of Assam brought upon the province than any other portion of it.

Such was the condition of Lakhimpur district before and during the British rule in Assam. The main roads in North Lakhimpur sub-division, as given by Hunter (1879:378) were Garmur, Kuchujan, Pathalipam, Dhakuakhana and Kherketia. The cost of maintenance of these roads during 1875-76 was much higher than the roads of other sub-divisions of the district. The total length of roads in the whole district was about 429 miles only. Hunter (1879:377) writes:

> .... besides these roads, the rivers form the only other means of communication. The large rivers detailed in a previous section of this Statistical Account, are open throughout the year, and thirty-five other minor streams are navigable during the rainy season.

And so far as Jonai area of the present Jonai sub-division is concerned, no mention has been made by him as there was no communication system with this area except by the rivers.

The district of Sibsagar (now Jorhat) from where the village Barpamua is taken for study, was more or less in the same situation in communication as that of Lakhimpur district. The principal lines of roads in Sibsagar district were the Trunk Roads, called the Seoni Ali, the Dhodar Ali, the Gar Ali, the Nawa Ali and so on. The bridge of the roads was mainly of bamboo and wood and, therefore, most of the roads were rendered impassable during the rains. The total length of roads in the district as shown by Hunter, (1879:258-59) was about 409 miles.

The improvement of roads in Assam is a recent phenomenon. Because only after the independence, construction and improvement of roads in Assam have taken place. At present, the length of roads under P.W.D. in Sibsagar district is 2909.18 Kms. and in Lakhimpur district, it is 948.01 Kms. (in 1970-71). In 1977 it has increased up to 3186:92 Kms. in Sibsagar district and 1043.95 Kms. in Lakhimpur district.[1] The length includes the black topped, gravelled, earthened roads of the two districts. The increasing figures of the lengths of the roads show the improvement of road transportation in Assam.

The villages of the present study have been getting the opportunity of road transportation recently. Improvement of roads in the Dhemaji and Jonai sub-divisions which includes Mohmora and Duhutimukh villages have been seen after the Chinese aggression of 1961-62. The village Mohmora of Jonai is situated to the north of the Jonai-Oiramghat P.W.D. road.[2] To the north-west, the same road connects the villages with Jonai, Murkongselek railway station and Jonai-Pashighat road. To the south-east, the road connects the village with Oiramghat, the ferryghat at the Brahmaputra, which links the area with Dibrugarh by water transport.

There is another road under construction from Jonai to Silapathar (a small town and railway station, west to Mohmora village) which is at the final phase of completion. These two are the principal roads which connect the village with the outer world. According to the villagers, they had not seen such improved roads twenty years back in their area. The road construction was spread up after the Chinese aggression in 1962. The second village Duhutimukh is connected by P.W.D. road with Dhemaji town and the northern Trunk Road of Assam. And from there another P.W.D. road started from the trunk road is connecting the village with Dhemaji railway station which is about five kilometres from the village. The P.W.D. road which is running across the village connected it with Sonarighat of the Brahmaputra through the Trunk Road which is further connected with Dibrugarh, the district headquarters of Dibrugarh district. There is another newly constructed road across the village running towards south-west which connects the village with Dhemaji town.

The village Barpamua of Majuli in Sibsagar district is situated about one kilometre west to the Kamalabari-Haldhibari P.W.D. road. It connects the village with Kamalabari, a small town of Majuli and with Jorhat, the district headquarter town of Sibsagar. The village is situated on the bank of the river Khersuti and a river dam across Khersuti is connecting the village with Dhakuakhana, Gugamukh, Lakhimpur town and other places of Lakhimpur district. After the earthquake of 1950 in Assam, the situation of transport communication has worsened. Practically only two motorable roads, viz., Kamalabari-Haldhibari and Kamalabari-Lakhimpur roads are there in Majuli. That too suffer during the summer season of every year. Anyhow, excluding the summer season, Barpamua, now-a-days, is well connected with the other parts of Majuli and outer world in the whole year.

Along with the construction of roads and development of transportation, the villagers have the opportunity to develop contact with the outer world. As a result, their attitudes, economy and culture have been changing day by day. However, the result of contact with the outer world due to improvement of road has not always been positive. In this context, Elwin (1964:74-75) writes from the logical point of view on NEFA (Arunachal Pradesh) as follows :

> Roads, of course, can be a curse as well as a blessing to the tribal people. In some places they have been the means of corruption and exploitation. They have brought new diseases, moral decline and cultural decadence. They have made it easy for the money-lenders, the rapacious merchants, the liquor-venders, the

> lawyer's tent to penetrate deep into the hills and forests. They can bring money in, but they can also take money out. They have helped to destroy the handloom industry by the import of cheap bazar cloth; they have brought vulgar and inferior goods to the very doors of the people.

Similarly, various changes have been taking place among the Mishings with the improvement of roads. At the very outset, the roads break the isolation of the tribal people. Along with the improvement of roads, they have moved from the stage of oral communication, signs and symbols to the modern written communication. The primitive system of communication and transportation were the messengers, boats and elephants. When roads were improved, the importance of these agents decreased. The messengers, boats and elephants were replaced by post and telegraph, buses, railways, taxis, jeeps etc. As a matter of fact, their range of communication has increased. The place of traditional messenger has been taken by post and telegraph. Similarly, the place of boats and elephants has been taken by buses and railways. Expansion of communication network is the cause of these changes.

The neighbours of the Mishings are Assamese speaking people. When they migrated from the hills of Arunachal to the plains of Assam, they had to learn Assamese for communication with the neighbouring people. As Assamese is the medium of instruction in schools and colleges, it helped later on to spread Assamese language among the Mishings. Now-a-days, all communications e.g., writing of letters among themselves are done in Assamese. Therefore, the sending of messages through messengers in Mishing language have been replaced by Assamese language. It has happened in terms of sending letters through postal services.

The growth of marketing centres like Dhemaji, Silapathar, Jonai in Dhemaji and Jonai sub-divisions, Kamalabari, Jengraimukh, Phulani in Majuli have been the result of improvements of roads and other means of communication. The marketing centres also widened the network of communication of the Mishings. They had started exchang of culture with neighbouring communities in terms of exchanging (selling and buying) agricultural products, domestic possessions in the market. As a result, market communication starts, introducing market economy among them. They now sell their surplus products in the market. So, along with the improvement of roads and growth of marketing centres, the traditional barter system and the primitive communication system are gradually extinguishing among them.

Availability of books, newspapers, radios in the nearby marketing centres help in the expansion of communication system of the Mishings. These are also replacing the primitive mode of sending messages of the Mishings. Now-a-days, books and newspapers are found easily in the market, the people are using these as means of mass-communication. As a result, the primitive isolation has been breaking. The folk tales and the folk songs have been replaced by radio listening and cinema. Now-a-days, in place of listening to the folk tales, the people use to listen radio programmes. Folk songs are becoming a part of occasional festivals due to the popularity of programmes of songs on radio.

The above mentioned factors are responsible for the replacement of oral communication of the Mishings. These are all happening due to the improvement of roads and transportation. As a result, the people became the part of the regional and national communication network. Moreover, due to the changes of the primitive types of communication to the modern communication system, gradually, deformation of the superstructure of the people started.

Introduction of Railways and its Impact

Since the introduction of railways in India during the time of Lord Dalhousie in the middle part of nineteenth century, India has seen a tremendous change in the field of transport communication.[3] Assam was not left behind from the facilities of railways as some of the major industries, *viz.*, tea, oil, coal etc., were developing under the British Government. Of course, the work of construction of railways was a difficult task as this region always suffers from heavy monsoons and floods (Saxena: 1962). At present the N.F. Railway in Assam has been well extended in the north-eastern region. But the broad gauge is still lying behind in comparison to metre gauge. In 1973-74 the route length of broad gauge (single) in Assam was only 105.22 kms., whereas length of metre gauge was 2088.43 kms. (including single and double routes).[4] The introduction of railways in the area under study is of recent origin. 154 kms. of railway track from North Lakhimpur to Murkongselek passes through the Mishing populated area. But construction of railway track from North Lakhimpur to Gogamukh was completed only in 1964 and from Gogamukh to Murkongselek in 1965. And the railways from North Lakhimpur to Murkongselek was practically opened only in February, 1966.[5] It is the only railway line in the north bank of the Brahmaputra valley.

The two villages, Mohmora and Duhutimukh of Lakhimpur district are getting enormous facilities from the railways as they are situated near the railway station. The village Mohmora is situated only 2 kms. away from Murkongselek railway station. The village Duhutimukh is about 5 kms. from Dhemaji railway station.[6] The villagers now have the facilities to develop social, economical and political links out of their own areas by railways.

Most of the villagers of Mohmora saw train for the first time in 1965-66. The introduction of railways up to Murkongselek is mainly for commercial purpose. The timber and other forest resources of the area and of Arunachal Pradesh have been transported to Lakhimpur and beyond through railways. The supply of essential commodities to these areas is possible only through railways. Due to this, the importance of Jonai is increasing day by day. As a result of it the isolation of the villagers has been broken to a greater extent. Due to the growth of marketing centres and facilities for transportation, the villagers found the place to sell their surplus agricultural products. As a matter of fact, they are playing a considerable part in regional as well as national economy. To a certain extent, the villagers are also helping in discovering and abstracting forest resources of the area which allow them to play a part in the national economy as well as global economy.

Apart from these, after the introduction of railways, immigrants started to move to the Mishing populated areas. New immigrants consist of mainly Bengalis, Beharis, Nepalese, Monipuris and Boro-Kacharis. For communication of ideas, it became a part of the Mishing way of life to learn the languages of the immigrants and *vice-versa*. In this process, the Mishings have learnt Assamese, Hindi, Bengali and Nepali languages. The first three are the main languages for communication in the Mishing populated areas. As a result, the Mishings learn to speak both Hindi and Bengali. They can speak or understand the languages of the other immigrants like the Nepalese and the Boro-Kacharis. As a matter of fact, the Mishings, now-a-days, can be regarded as multi-lingual group.

Moreover, interaction between the Mishings and the immigrants have taken place. It has helped in exchanging cultures of all the newly arrived communities and the Mishings. Exchange of culture has taken place both in the forms of ideas and elements. These would not have happened without the introduction of railways.

The railways broke the isolation of the Mishings. It was mentioned earlier about the primitive form of communication of the Mishings and their isolation from the modern world. The railways not only replaced the primitive form of communication system, but also broke their isolation. Due to the railways, the people now-a-days, can move from one place to another in cheap fare. The social, cultural, economical and political life of the Mishings is no longer confined to them only. By some way or the other, they became the part of the regional communication system. Therefore, railways have not been breaking their isolation, but also affecting the compactness of the Mishing community.

The range of communication of the Mishings has enlarged with the introduction of railways. Now-a-days, the Mishings can go to the places where they like. In Lakhimpur district, the Mishing villagers get much comfort in going by train than by other means of transportation. Train journey is cheaper and better for them. Like the replacement of primitive agents of communication by roads, railways also help in replacing majority of the agents. The learning of different languages, the interaction and movement of the people are the examples of enlargement of range of communication of the Mishings.

A paradigm of communication network as given shall indicate the form, technique, institution, range etc., of communication system of the Mishings.

Impact of the Marketing Centres

The type of marketing centres in tribal setting is of great importance (see Dewey, 1962; Sinha, 1968), since they provide meeting place for economic and cultural exchange in the surrounding area. The three villages, namely Mohmora, Duhutimukh and Barpamua have been getting marketing facilities to a great extent. Jonai is the nearest centre for the villagers of Mohmora. Moreover, other small marketing places of Bahir Jonai, Laimekuri etc. are there which are held once a week. Apart from these marketing centres, the villagers also go to the major marketing centres like Pashighat, Silapathar and Dhemaji. Some of the major marketing centres enjoyed by the villagers of Duhutimukh are Dhemaji, Jiadhal, Maridhal, Gugamukh and others. The villagers of Barpamua of Majuli have also several marketing places, they are Jengraimukh Tinali, Ratanpur, Phulani, Garmur, Kamalabari and others. The villagers go to these marketing places to sell their agricultural products, domestic possessions and to purchase their domestic requirements. These marketing places are significant for the people where they come into contact with traders and customers of different places. Two main languages, viz.,

PARADIGM : 1

COMMUNICATION NETWORK OF THE MISHINGS

Sl. No.	Form	Technique	Institutions/Way	Range	Transportation/ Agents	Languages used	Approx. period/periods
1.	Oral communication (Intra-community)	Personal (face to face, importance on primary relationship)	Kebang, Murong, Barik, Deka Bora etc.	Intra-village. Inter-village	Boats, Elephants, Messengers	Mishing dialect	15th to 17th Century A.D.
2.	Oral communication (Inter-community)	Personal (face to face, importance in relationship) Impersonal (secondary relationship)	Namghar, Satra	Inter-community (Regional)	Boats, Elephants, Messengers	Mishing dialect. Broken Assamese	17th to 19th Century A.D
3.	Written (Mass-communication)	Personal (face to face) Impersonal (Importance on secondary relationship)	School, College, Marketing centres	Regional National International	Newspaper, Magazine, Radio, Cinema, P & T etc.	Mishing dialect, Assamese, Hindi, Bengali, English etc.	20th Century
4.	Transport communication	Personal Impersonal (Importance on secondary relationship)	Roads, Railways	Regional National	Bus, Train, Taxi, Motor, Cycle etc.	–do–	–do–

Assamese and Hindi are generally used for commercial purposes in the marketing centres. They rarely use their own dialect or Bengali.

Some of the significant changes due to marketing centres are as follows:

(1) Few years back, the people did not produce surplus agricultural products for commercial purposes. The main drawback was the lack of marketing centres. Now, they try to produce as much as possible so that the surplus agricultural products can be sold in the market. Moreover, domestic possessions like pig, fowl etc. are also sold, now-a-days, in the market to meet their daily needs.

(2) As a matter of fact, in the light of the above situation the subsistence economy of the Mishing villagers gradually has been transferred into the market economy. The people now no longer depend upon the barter for exchange of goods and materials.

(3) Due to the exchange of language and culture with the non-tribal people, the emergence of petty entrepreneurship among the villagers is seen. They are now engaged in petty business and shop-keeping in the marketing places.

These are some of the effects of the marketing centres on the villagers under study. In some cases the effect of the marketing centre is so deep that some of the villagers often tried to show off and behave as the Marwaries of their respective places. It may lead to further changes among them in future.

Impact of Post & Telegraph, Radio Listening and Newspaper Reading

In the field of communication, mass media have been playing an important role even among the illiterate tribal people. If not directly, at least indirectly, it effects them. Therefore, mass-media are highly essential in communicating even the preliterate people (see Elselein and Topper : 1976). But unfortunately the villagers have not sufficiently adopted mass media and have not properly learned to utilise them. The three villages under study have been getting the facilities of post and telegraph. The offices are located at Jonai, Dhemaji and Jengraimukh. Still then due to less utilisation of mass media, the possessions like radio, newspaper etc. are less among the respondents. The following table shows the same :

Table 6.1

Educational Qualification and Use of Mass Media

Educational Qualification	Use of Mass Media			Row Total
	Newspaper	Radio	No Possession	
Illiterate	—	13 10.00 20.01	117 90.00	130 100.00
Literate	2 1.23 33.33	38 13.45 58.46	122 75.32	162 100.00
Undermatric	2 6.06 33.33	10 30.30 15.38	21 63.64	33 100.00
Matriculate and above	2 20.00 33.34	4 40.00 6.15	4 40.00	10 100.00
Column Total	6 100.00	65 100.00	264 100.00	335 100.00

The above table indicates that out of the 130 illiterate respondents 13 (10.00%) have radio; distribution of radio sets among the other groups of respondents is as follows–33 (23.85%) out of 162 literates, 10 (30.30%) out of 33 undermatrics and 4 (40.00%) out of 10 matriculates and above. The newspaper subscribers are very rare but still found among the literates. Out of 162 literates, only 2 (1.23%) respondents subscribe to newspapers.

During the course of field work, it was found that though newspaper, radio and other possessions of mass communication are less, the limited possessions have been influencing the people significantly. The impact can be summarised as follows :

(1) Though newspaper subscribers are very few among the respondents, one or two daily newspapers are sufficient for the whole village; because the household of the people are very close to each other and a literate person is quite sufficient to tell them the daily happenings. It leads to two major effects. Firstly, the daily evening assembly of the villagers in a certain household helps them to understand each other which leads to greater co-operation. Secondly, they can sort out some necessary problems in the newspapers.

(2) Possession of radio has also two fold effects on them. Firstly, the light programmes (drama, song etc.) which, for them, is

one of the main sources of recreation after so much of daily hard labour. Secondly, it has been helping the people to gather daily news. Of course, in some cases, it was found that the possession of radio is a matter of luxury for the well to do families.

Interaction and Communication with Religious, Political and Educational Elites

Communication through leaders is of significant value at the village level. The village level leaders are usually of two types, viz., the illiterate village heads or religious heads and the political and educated elites (teachers, businessmen and the Government employees). The village heads help in maintaining customs and traditions, administering the village and thereby maintain peace and order within the village. Contrary to it, the educated leaders help the villagers to come into contact with modern way of life. These two types of leaders are found in the villages under study. In Mohmora, it is found that the illiterate and the semi-literate elder villagers are much more active in comparison to other co-villagers. In Duhutimukh and Barpamua, the educated villagers who are engaged in business and service are found leading the people on socio-economic and socio-political links. These link the people with outer world through meetings, discussions and suggestions. In this context, the students have also been playing an important role. The students studying in schools and colleges at Jonai, Dhemaji and Jengraimukh help the people to gather new ideas in various fields. During the course of field work, it was found that the elder village leaders and the students are active and expressive. The following are the main contributions of leaders and students to the villagers:

(1) The new ideas are practically accepted by the villagers only after seeking proper clarifications. They develop confidence in new ideas and enterprises if they are approved by the leaders.

(2) The illiterate elders like to listen to their educated children. Therefore, modern ideas are finding entry into the Mishing villages through educated youths.

(3) Thus, discussions and suggestions of the leaders and students are playing an important role in these villages and they are developing new links with the outside world.

III

In conclusion of this chapter, some of the personal views of the respondents on the influence of communication to the people are given below

Case Study 6.1

Name - Shri Kanta Doley. Age–65 years. He does not own a radio set and does not subscribe a newspaper. As informed by Shri Doley of Barpamua village, during the time of his youth, oral communication was the only means of communication among them. Intra-village communications were done by the messengers and the inter-village communications were managed through the messengers who travelled either by boat, elephant or on foot. According to him, face to face relationship was maintained by maintaining oral tradition. There were no written records of the proceedings of the *Kebang*, *Murong*, *Namghar* of the village. Even the *Gosains* of the *Satras* converted and taught them the *Kewal-Dharma* orally. Now, he has seen tremendous changes in the field of communication. He talked proudly of his capability to move from one place to another due to transport facilities. He is also happy in getting personal messages in terms of letters from his distant relatives. In connection with the elites, he said that they were very helpful for the illiterate villagers like him and informed us about the happenings in the outer world. They discuss various matters in the religious institution (*Namghar*) with the religious leaders when *pujas* and festivals are held. Political and educated elites of their villages inform them news either in terms of gossip or discussion.

Case Study 6.2

Name - Shri Bidya Paw. Age-29 years. He subscribes a newspaper and owns a radio set. Shri Paw, a villager of Mohmora, is of the opinion that since the introduction of railways in the year 1964-65, they have been getting better communication facilities. The entire atmosphere of Jonai area has changed due to the arrival of the immigrants. They get benefit in communicating themselves with the Hindi and Bengali speaking people.

There is a radio in his family. He told that radio listening has become his habit. His most popular items are the local news, Mishing programmes, other light programmes on songs and drama. The languages of the programmes are mainly Assamese and Hindi. His co-villagers use to visit his residence for listening to radio.

Table 6.2

Differential levels of Communication in Three Villages

Village	Total Respondents	Number of radio sets owned by the respondents	Ratio of ownership of radio : respondents	Number of newspaper subscribed by the respondents	Ratio of the subscription of newspapers : respondents
Village I : Mohmora (Jonai)	106	20	1 : 5.3	1	1 : 106
Village II : Duhutimukh (Dhemaji)	45	16	1 : 2.8	2	1 : 22.5
Village III Barpamua (Majuli)	148	29	1 : 6.3	3	1 : 61.3

Case Study 6.3

Name - Lakheswar Kardong. Age–32 years. He subscribes one Assamese daily and owns a transistor set.

Keeping in view the importance of mass media, he started a cinema hall in Dhemaji in 1969. According to him, though it was a business, yet his aim was to educate the local villagers by showing few good pictures. The news and knowledge gathered from radio and newspaper are usually explained by him to the illiterate villagers. Accordingly, he tries to inform to the villagers reading the events in other areas. He says that radio and newspapers, now-a-days, are easily available in the market. Shri Kardong is of the opinion that if transport communication and mass media are used properly by his co-villagers, it will help in their socio-economic and political development.

On the basis of our field observation, primary data and the case studies we can derive the following conclusions regarding the differential levels of communication in the three villages under study :

(1) According to table 6.2, it has been found that in gross terms, there are radio sets in the village Barpamua but if we try to analyse the radio then the position is much better in Duhutimukh where there is one radio set for 2.8 respondents.

(2) As regards the subscription of newspapers, the position is again much better in Duhutimukh where one newspaper is subscribed for a group of 22.5 respondents.

References

1 Source : Statistical Handbook of Assam, 1971, 1976.

2 The situation of the villages has been discussed in Chapter III of this dissertation. In this chapter slight repetition is made for the determination of communication facilities of the villages.

3 See 'Indian Railways : Rates and Regulations' by N.B. Mehta, 1927, P.S. King and Son Ltd., London; and 'Indian Railways' by A. Prasad, 1960, Asia Publishing House, Bombay.

4 Source : Statistical Handbook of Assam, 1976.

5 Source : Note Book of Survey and Construction Organization of N.F. Railway, which is obtained from Maligaon, Guwahati, Headquarter at Kurseng in the district of Darjeeling, West Bengal.

6 The village Barpamua of Majuli has got no railway facilities as it is situated in the river island Majuli of Sibsagar district. A comparative study in the process of discussion will be made in the next chapter while the question of development with the help of the two variables: acculturation and communication will arise.

Damle, Dr. Y.B.
1965 Communication of Modern Ideas and Knowledges in Indian Villages. Deccan College, Poona (India).

Das, B.M.
1967 Assamese Culture and the Hill People of North-Eastern India. In R. Mitra and B. Das Gupta (eds.), A common perspective of North-East India. Calcutta, Pannalal Das Gupta.

Elwin, Verrier
1964 A Philosophy for NEFA, Shillong.

Elselein, E.B. and M. Topper.
1976 Media Anthropology. A Theoretical Framework. Human Organization 2, Vol. 5, Summer.

Furer-Haimendorf, Christoph von
1939 The Naked Nagas. London : Routledge and Kegan Paul.

Gorer, Geoffrey
1938 Himalayan Village : An Account of Lepchas of Sikkim (with an introduction by J.H. Hutton). London : Michael, Josheph.

Hunter, W.W.
1879 A Statistical Account of Assam. Vol. II. Trubner & Co., London. Reprinted 1975 by B.R. Publishing Corporation, Delhi.

Hockings, Paul
1977 Communication Networks. In M.N. Srinivas, S. Seshaiah and V.S. Parthasarathy (eds.), Dimensions of Social Change in India. Allied Publishers Pvt. Ltd., Bombay.

Hutton, J.
1921 The Angami Nagas. London : Macmillan.

Lionberger, Herbert F. and B.A. Heddy
1976 Reference Group Influence on Extension Communication of Social Science Faculty. Rural Sociology I Vol. 41, Spring.

Mishra, V.M.
1973 The Communication Media and Learning for Modernization : A Conceptual Model. Indian Journal of Social Research 2, Vol. XIV, August.

Majumder, D.N.
1967 Social Organization of the Koch of Garo Hills. In Rathin Mitra, B. Das Gupta (eds.), A Common Perspective of North-East India. Calcutta : Pannalal Das Gupta.

Robinson, W.
1841 A Descriptive Account of Assam. Reprinted 1975 by Sanskaran Prakashak, Delhi.

Roy Burman, B.K. and S.P. Thakral
1970 Demographic and Socio-economic Profiles of the Hill Areas of North-East India. Census of India 1961, New Delhi : Office of the Registrar General of India.

Saxena, K.K.
1962 Indian Railways : Problems and Prospects. Vora & Co. Publishers Pvt. Ltd., Bombay 2.

Sinha, D.P.

1968 Cultural Change in an Intertribal Market. Asia Publishing House, New Delhi.

Sinha, Raghubir.

1962 The Akas. Shillong : Research Department, Advisers Secretariat.

CHAPTER VII

SOCIO-ECONOMIC DEVELOPMENT

I

In this chapter, our main focus is to analyse the nature of socio-economic development among the Mishings. The Mishings as a community have passed through several stages of development. At first, they were hill-dwellers. At that stage, their economy consisted of food gathering, hunting and fishing. They moved to the plains of the Brahamputra Valley and came in contact with permanently settled Assamese villagers. The physical mobility (movement from the hill to the plains) and cultural contact with the Assamese peasantry brought about a great deal of economic and cultural change among them. They developed semi-permanent settlement and started shifting (*Jhoom*) cultivation along with hunting and fishing. At this stage their production was entirely for the purpose of consumption (Dubey : 1978).

The growing contact with Assamese peasantry has its bearing over the Mishings and they developed their permanent settlement in the form of villages, adopted permanent cultivation and gradually discarded shifting cultivation. Now, in many areas, their agricultural products are surplus and almost in every village, some of the families are engaged in trade, business, contract and service. A few of them are professionals. Of late a number of Indian studies on tribes have tried to show the relationship between physical mobility, social interaction, acculturation and change in economic organisation (Rao : 1966; Sinha : 1968; Aurora: 1972; Dubey: 1978). Some of the Indian sociologists tried to analyse the impact of communication on Indian villages (Damle: 1955). Some of the sociologists and anthropologists have focused their attention on the question of tribal development (Sinha: 1972; Vidyarthi and Rai: 1976; Kulkarni : 1976). The main focus of the present chapter is to probe into the following issues :

(a) The physical mobility in the case of a community brings it into the contact with other communities. This process leads to increased interaction and acculturation.

(b) The acculturation and communication bring about change in the economic organisation of a community. This is visible in the case of Mishings also. Their productive techniques, occupational structure, nature of production (from subsistence to surplus), investment pattern, concept of health, schooling have undergone considerable change.

As regards the first issue, we have discussed in details in other chapters and in the first page of this chapter. The historical structural relationship between acculturation, communication and development in the case of Mishings is explained through the help of paradigm.

It was mentioned in the fifth chapter that acculturation has taken place in different aspects of the social life of the Mishings. The *Donyee-Polo* worshippers now-a-days, regard themselves as Hindu and their religion is known as *Kewalia, Kalhanghati* or *Nisamalia*. It was, however, observed during the field work that both acculturation and communication have started motivating the people to acquire new techniques of production, to receive new ideas, to adopt innovations and to send their children to schools and colleges. It was found that the processes of acculturation and communication have made people conscious for greater sense of equality and respect for human dignity.

The acculturation and communication have accelerated the pace of development. Now, the Mishings as a community are not isolates. They are linked with their neighbours, regional culture and nation through Hinduism, mythology, Assamese and Hindi languages, railways and marketing system. The process of democratic decentralisation has aroused tremendous political consciousness among the Mishings. This can be proved by their participation in elections and positions occupied by them in the State level hierarchy of the different political parties. The improved nature of social development is visible among them through the spread of modern education, growth of educational institutions, availability of medical facilities and access to modern channels of communications.

In the political sphere too, acculturation and communication have been playing influential roles. The *Murong* and *Kebang* have gradually been losing their status as decision making body of the people. As observed in the field, the newly emerged leaders are replacing the traditional leaders and the former are more and more alert in acquiring new knowledge and ideas. And for maintaining their position and status they

PARADIGM : 2

LEVELS OF DEVELOPMENT AMONG THE MISHINGS

1		2	3	4
1.	Migration	From Hills to Plains	Semi-permanent Settlement	Permanent Settlement
2.	Acculturation	(a) Tribal beliefs, customs, traditional form of worship. (b) Own dialect (c) Own institutions, Kebang, Murong etc.	(a) Contact with Assamese and Gosains of Satras (b) Use of broken Assamese language (c) Assimilation started	(a) Converted into Nisamalia Dharma (b) Namghar, Satra become part of culture. (c) Growth of different sects. (d) Multi-lingual group. (e) Institution like Murong became less important.
3.	Communication	(a) On foot (b) Oral communication (Intra-community)	(a) Oral communication (Intra-community & intern-community) (b) Boats, elephants, messengers	(a) Mass communication (P&T, radio, books, newspapers etc.) (b) Transport communication (Train, Bus, Taxi, etc.)
4.	Development (Economy, health, education)	(a) Food gathering, hunting, fishing (b) Faith in village medicine manmagic, supernatural powers (c) Much literacy	(a) Cultivation similar to shifting cultivation (b) Production entirely for consumption (c) Faith in village medi-Cine-man, magic, super-natural power (d) Semi-literate	(a) Permanent cultivation. (b) Surplus productions sell in marketing centres. (c) People engaged in business, contract, service. (d) Decline of importance of medicineman. (e) Faith in modern medical treatment. (f) Schools, Colleges established. (g) Literacy increased, qualified persons available.

have been trying to improve their information level. In the same way acculturation and communication have been helping simultaneously in the field of political participation and in knowing the Government plans and programmes.

Thus, both acculturation and communication are responsible for the socio-cultural changes and the development of the people under study. The influence of both the variables is accepted by the people unanimously. During the time of field work, few of the respondents expressed their views on the role of acculturation and communication which are given in the following case studies :

Case Study 7.1

Name—Shri Maghar Paw. Age—70 years. Village—Mohmora.

Shri Paw, who migrated to Mohmora in the early sixties, expressed that even before his migration, he had observed the socio-cultural changes occurring in his community. "But", as he says, "I do not know how it can be determined. Changes are no doubt due to, as you say, acculturation and communication and by other means. But the main fact behind is the demand of time". Thus, he has given stress on the 'time factor' which is leading his community towards socio-cultural changes.

Case Study 7.2

Name - Shri Samburam Kardong. Age - 55 years. Village Duhutimukh.

As he told, since the migration of their family from Dihingmukh of Sibsagar district in the early part of this century, they have been in constant contact with Assamese people. Before migration to this village, they adopted several socio-cultural patterns of the non-tribal-Assamese. He said that their migration itself indicates the impact of communication and then acculturation.

According to him, the acceptance of *Kewalia* or *Nisamalia* cult of Hinduism from the *Gosains* of the *Satras* was the first step of their socio-cultural change. He said that continuous structural changes of the Mishing society is due to the improvement of communication system in all spheres.

II

During the British period and prior to it, the socio-economic condition of the villagers under study was much backward. There was no proper system of transportation, and no educated people were in the villages. Only after the improvement in transportation and the impact of acculturation, the economy of the people has been gradually developing to a certain extent.

The villagers under study are essentially agriculturists. Some of the main agricultural products of the people are paddy, mustard seeds, black pulse, jute, potato and some other vegetables. The main crop is the paddy. The people grow three types of paddy, i.e. *Sali, Ahu* and *Bao*. As informed by the villagers under study, *Bao* (suitable for marshy and swampy land), was the only paddy cultivated by them prior to the Independence of India. The introduction of cultivation of *Sali* and *Ahu* was of recent origin. Both varieties are now popular among them. Contrary to the production of paddy, mustard seeds and black pulse, productions are very limited. The villagers are essentially agriculturists. Due to the process of acculturation and communication, the occupational structure of the people is changing gradually.[1] Now, few of the villagers are engaged in other occupations also, e.g. government service, business and contract. The following table indicates the occupation of the respondents.

Table 7.1

Occupation of the Respondents

Occupation	Total	Percentage
Cultivation	315	94.06
Government Service	15	4.47
Any other (Business and others)	5	1.47
Total	335	100.00

The above table indicates that the villagers under study are mostly agriculturists. Agriculture is the main occupation of 315 (94.06%) respondents. Contrary to it, only 15(4.47%) are in government services and 5(1.47%) are engaged in other occupations like business, daily labour and others. Even though the percentage of occupation of the respondents other than agriculture is small, it signifies the gradual transformation of occupation of the people.[2]

In spite of main occupation, the respondents possessed subsidiary occupations also. Though comparatively less in number, most of the respondents under study are in favour of subsidiary occupations for the maintenance of their family. Here the impact of acculturation and communication may be because of economic necessity, but the people learn it only after the contact with the non-tribals. That can be proved by the following table which indicates the subsidiary occupations of three generations of the respondents including their own:

Table 7.2

Subsidiary Occupation of Three Generations of the Respondents' Family

Generation	Subsidiary occupation		No subsidiary occupation	Total
	Cultivation	Business		
Grandfather	—	11 3.28	324 96.72	335 100.00
Father	—	26 7.75	309 92.25	335 100.00
Self	17 5.07	131 39.10	187 55.83	335 100.00

According to the above table, it is seen that 11 (3.28%) out of the grandfathers of 335 respondents had business as their subsidiary occupation and 324 (96.72%) had no subsidiary occupation. The number was raised to a certain extent during the time of the fathers of the respondents where 26 (7.75%) had subsidiary occupation. So far as the respondents of the present study are concerned, 17(5.07%) have cultivation as subsidiary occupation and 13(39.10%) respondents have business as their subsidiary occupation. What it indicates is that the villagers under study are gradually less inclined on land and alternatively they are taking subsidiary occupations for economic self-sufficiency.

From the discussion of the occupations of the respondents it has been proved again that the main occupation of the villagers is agriculture. While the question of agriculture is there, the question of use of modern methods in agriculture will also be there. In this context, how acculturation and communication are playing their roles is significant. The less use of modern methods of agriculture is highly connected with their culture. (Doley: 1973; Bhandari: 1974) But it has been changing due to the gradual change in their attitude and the communication through Government plans and programmes. However, the agricultural methods and implements of the respondents are similar to those of the non-tribal Assamese. The villagers mainly depend on bullocks, plough and axes in cultivation.

As observed in the field, the respondents use their own method for the fertility of the land. They burn the weeds and shrubs of the fallow land.

Its ashes are used as fertilizer, therefore, their cultivation in fallow land is seen to be shifting to *Jhoom* cultivation, and of course, because of that, Hunter (1879) once regarded them as nomadic agriculturists. While on discussion, the people informed that these practices are common among them is not because of their traditional habit but due to the constant disturbance caused by floods and erosions. In spite of these, modern methods of cultivation, e.g. use of fertilizer, insecticide etc. are used by the respondents in their cultivation. The use of modern methods for much agricultural outputs is, however, not so popular among them. Therefore the popularity of modern methods of cultivation does not vary in the families irrespective of rich and poor. Table 7.3 indicates the same. The table shows that out of the 21 respondents, who used chemical fertilizers in their cultivation, 9(42.86%) are self-sufficient and 12(57.14%) are lacking from self-sufficiency. Similarly, out of 124 respondents who used insecticides, 50(40.32%) are self-sufficient and 74(59.68%) are not economically sound, but still then they accepted the methods of use of insecticides in their cultivation. Other modern methods wherever possible are accepted by the people. The table indicates that all the methods are equally popular irrespective of rich and poor.

Table 7.3

Agricultural Innovation and Self-sufficiency

Modern Methods	Self-sufficiency		Row Total
	Yes	No	
Chemical Fertilizers	9 42.86 5.14	12 57.14 7.50	21 100.00
Insecticides	50 40.32 28.32	74 59.68 46.25	124 100.00
Varieties of Methods	56 71.79 32.00	22 28.21 13.75	78 100.00
Dont't use	60 53.57 34.29	52 46.43 32.50	112 100.00
Column Total	175 100.00	160 100.00	335 100.00

It can, however, be said from the above discussion that acculturation and communication motivate the respondents to accept the modern methods of cultivation. The same are motivating the respondents, who are not self-sufficient, to accept alternative means to maintain their families. It may not be regarded strictly as economic development but still it can be regarded as the change of attitude of the people towards economy. Various other alternatives now-a-days are taken by the villagers under study for their livelihood which can be proved from the following table:

Table 7.4

Alternatives to Maintain the Family of the Respondents

Self-sufficiency	Alternatives					Row Total
	Daily Labour	Business	Service	Cottage industry	Varieties of Alternatives	
Yes	—	—	—	—	—	175 100.00
No	25 15.62 100.00	84 52.50 100.00	5 3.13 100.00	—	46 28.75 100.00	160 100.00
Column Total	25 100.00	84 100.00	5 100.00		46 100.00	335 100.00

From the table, it is found that out of the 160 respondents, who have not much agricultural productions for self-sufficiency, 25(15.62%) are engaged in daily labour, 84(52.50%) are in business, 5(3.13%) are in service and 46(28.75%) are taking varieties of alternatives to maintain their families. It is to be noted here that the beggar's problem is gradually increasing in rural Assam. But among the poor respondents under study, no such instances are found. Even by adopting job like daily labour, the people tried to maintain their status and self-sufficiency. It is, of course, the economic motives of the people in making a living of their own.

As indicated earlier, both acculturation and communication are helping in economic motivations of villagers which lead to the gradual economic development of the people. Due to the change in attitude and contact with non-tribal Assamese and businessmen, the people now have the knowledge to invest their incomes according to the needs of the family. Formerly, agricultural production, which was the sole factor of income, was used primarily for consumption only. But now-a-days, as observed in the field, the villagers have various means of income to raise the economic status of the family. According to the learning of sources of income, they now learn to invest their income also. The primary investment of the income of the respondents is in consumption and in the education of their children. It is found logical while the respondents were asked to give preferences on the sources of investment of their income. The table given below indicates the same.

Table 7.5

Preferences Given by the Respondents in the Investment of their Inome

	Source of Investment	Preferences					Total
		1st	2nd	3rd	4th	5th	
1.	In cultivation for more production	40 11.94	117 34.92	164 48.97	14 4.17	—	335 100.00
2.	Only for consumption	138 41.22	108 32.23	89 26.55	—	—	335 100.00
3.	For the education of the children	153 45.69	98 29.25	62 18.50	22 6.56	—	335 100.00
4.	Only for enjoyment	—	8 2.38	17 5.07	282 84.20	28 9.35	335 100.00
5.	Any other (for medical treatment and other domestic purpose.)	47 14.02	35 10.44	23 6.86	82 24.47	148 44.21	335 100.00

According to the table cited above, the highest number of respondents have first preference to their investment on the education of the children. Here, out of 335 respondents 153 (45.69%) have preferred first to invest their income for the education of their children. The second highest first preference of investment of income is given on consumption. Out of the 335 respondents 138 (41.22%) have preferred first to invest their income for consumption only. If the table is analysed carefully, it can be found out that the people have given preference according to the need of the investment of their income. It further proved that the people, nowadays, give much more stress on the education of their children. The motivation behind it is to raise their social and economic status simultaneously.

In connection with the above discussion, few below.

Case Study 7.4

Name - Shri Mante Saro. Age - 45 years. Village - Mohmora.

According to Shri Saro's opinion, the economic development of his community is essentially based on acculturation and communication. He says, "Due to the changes in some of the Mishing traditional customs, our co-villagers are now eager to produce surplus agricultural products and sell them in the marketing centres. Few domestic possessions are also sold in the market. And we are happy that all type of communications, specially the improvement in transportation, help us to sell the surplus agricultural products or purchase essential commodities from other parts of the area.

Case Study 7.5

Name - Shri Moni Padun. Age - 60 years. Village - Duhutimukh.

Shri Padun is of the opinion that due to constant contact with not-tribal Assamese, the socio-economic structure of the Mishings has been changing. In comparison to the time of his youth, now-a-days, more status is given to the economically sound families. It leads to the determination of stratification system among them. Therefore, people are now conscious in producing more agricultural products to gain position in society. Ultimately, as he says, competition starts among the villagers for more agricultural output. He is of the opinion that it has paved the way for economic soundness among his co-villagers.

Case Study 7.6

Name-Shri Manuram Doley. Age-66 years. Village - Barpamua.

As informed by Shri Doley, majority of his co-villagers are self-sufficient. Their agricultural products are mostly for consumption. The profit gained out of selling surplus products is invested in the education of their children. Their community is changing gradually due to acculturation and communication. As a result, expenditure in various aspects has been increasing. Therefore, as he told, the villagers are bound to do business and to take other alternative measures to maintain their family. It leads to the division of labour among them. So, their sources of income have widened.

Health

The traditional notion about diseases of the people under study is that there are unknown spirits behind all kinds of diseases suffered by them. For the prevention of unknown diseases they worship their ancestors with *pujas* like *Dobur*, *Dotgang*, *Urom Apin* etc. The thunder and lightening (*Mukling-Taleng*), earth and water (*Among-Ashi*), air and fire (*Esar-Emi*) alike are believed to be spiritual beings possessing power greater than those of man. According to the belief of the people, they are benevolent to human beings, protect their farms and families from damages and misfortune, but they have to be kept appeased with occasional offerings called *Taleng-Uyu* and *Bokpu-Done* (eater of white cock). The evil spirits to whom every illness or misfortune is attributed are the spirits looking around the streams (*Ashi-Uyu*), the mountains (*Adi-Uyu*), the forest (*Yumrang-Uyu*) etc. To protect themselves from these spirits or *Uyus* they perform *pujas* for the respective *Uyus*. The *Miboo* is supposed to know the spirit or *Uyu* responsible for illness or trouble and the form of worship that will appease them. The *Miboo* or village expert, for instance, has often been found offering chickens in the name of *Dopum Dorum*, a demon having three heads, to evade the attack of tetanic or infantile convulsions and at times the spirit is threatened with heated iron-rod and burning pepper. These malevolent motives of the evil spirit (*Aiman Uyu*) causing bodily illness or misfortune have to be brought off by offering pig, fowl, plantains, Apong etc. in ways prescribed by the *Miboo* and expert (Pegu, 1956:56-57).

The *Dobur-Uyu* is one of the important ritual performance of the Mishings marked by its peculiar principles carried out with much rigidity. Women are debarred from attending it, and the occasion of parturition and menstruation, the two things related to women are taken to be most unauspicious, and they have to move away from the village compound before the day breaks. Traffic and business transaction with the neighbouring villages are held up completely for the day, and to that end significant sign-posts are pitched on the main gate ways of the village compound. Trespassing and misdemeanour are dealt with temporary confinement or retention of valuables till the performance is over.

In the morning, they approach each house demanding dues *Ajeng* and the family reciprocates by offering *Apong*, fowl, pig, and rice which they collect in a place in the outskirt of the village. Two idols simulating snake swallowing and egg, are prepared from some fern (*Buktok*) and split bamboo, and placed in the altar facing the rising sun. Pigs and fowls are sacrificed uttering some prayers meaning "Oh mother sun, father moon, Oh Divine Self, be pleased with these offerings and bless us with health and happiness" etc.

The queries on the origin and indication of these idols have been answered in most unqualified way. But it is the widely shared belief that the snake represents the Earth as an eternal source of life while the egg represents life itself with the potential power of manifestation. It reminds us of the snake pillar found in some ruins and reinstalled in the political officers' bungalow at Sadiya and the faint reference made in legends wherein the Pasi-Miyong have been alleged to have pleaded for the mercy of Padams who plundered their homestead in a war, to spare at least the snake-image. Though nothing could be taken as conclusive, it may be safely said that it has its origin in remote past and have come down since the details being lost in its antiquity.

Ancestor-worship is a common feature of their annual functions. The ancestors (*Urom-posum*) are held responsible for the health and happiness of the family members, and incurring displeasure to them may result in accident or some uncommon occurrence. To keep them pleased at their abode (*Uii-Among*) pigs and fowls are sacrificed after the ingathering of their crops. The Mishings believe that the departed souls reside at *Sine-Mobo* (abode of dead) from where they use to visit their near and dear ones; but their visits instead of being beneficent usually result in a catastrophe, most malicious, of them being those who met unnatural death. They have no clear idea, however, of the soul being reborn, but it is often heard to have said so and so has been reborn when they find some similarity between departed one and a new born baby (Pegu: 1956).

The diseases suffered by the people of the three villages under study are common with other neighbouring villages. Formerly, they frequently suffered from cholera due to the lack of drinking water facilities and other unhygienic conditions. The name *silo-siko* near Barpamua village which is mentioned in the discussions of the historical background of the village, is the example of the effect of cholera on the villagers. There was no primary health centre in and around the villages and those who could not survive from indigenous treatment succumbed to illness irrespective of whether it was serious or not.

At present, the villagers of Mohmora have been enjoying the facilities of ten-bedded hospital which is situated at Jonai. Similar facilities are enjoyed by the villagers of Duhutimukh from Dhemaji Civil Hospital and the villagers of Barpamua from Jengraimukh State Dispensary. In Barpamua village, there is an M.B.B.S. Doctor and three nurses in service from whom the villagers get advice from time to time.

Due to the medical facilities and the gradual increase of faith in medical treatment, the role of the magician-cum-medicineman or the *Miboo* has been declining among the villagers. Now-a-days, drinking water facilities like tube wells, ponds etc., are found in all the villages. Having all the essential facilities for maintaining health, death rate due to various diseases has been decreasing among the villagers.

The villagers are still in favour of extended family system. They favour the family with 20 to 25 members. Moreover, the villagers are of the opinion that for the increase of population of the Mishing community, high fertility of the women is essential. Therefore, most of them are not in favour of family planning. Two main causes for the dislike of family planning are: their weakness in large extended family system and the requirement of manpower is agricultural activities. Therefore, even though they like medical treatment their attitude towards family planning has been found to be invariably negative. Table 7.6 indicates the same. As shown in the table, out of 159 respondents, 50 (31.45%) from Mohmora, 30 (18.87%) from Duhutimukh and 79 (49.68%) from Barpamua like scientific medical treatment but they do not know much about family planning. It is found that out of 106 respondents who do not get family planning facilities, 40 (37.74%) respondents are from Mohmora, 5 (4.72%) are from Duhutimukh and 49 (46.23%) are from Barpamua respectively like medical facilities. Contrary to it, 4 (3.77%) respondents from Mohmora, 2 (1.89%) from Duhutimukh and 6 (5.65%) from Barpamua village are on medical treatment and also neutral in family planning schemes as they do not get facilities. Out of 70 respondents, 12 (17.14%) from Mohmora, 8 (11.43%) from Duhutimukh and 50 (71.43%) from Barpamua like medical treatment but they do not like family planning. The table indicates that most of the respondents of the three villages under study are in favour of modern medical treatment but family planning is not popular among them. As mentioned earlier, the main reason behind the unpopularity of birth control is the requirement of manpower in their agricultural activities. In spite of so many changes, cultural drawback and illiteracy have also been playing a major role in the unpopularity of family planning scheme among the villagers.

Education

The education of the villagers of this study is satisfactory. Satisfactory in the sense that though the respondents are mostly illiterates, their children are qualified or at least literate. It is mainly due to the L.P. schools

Table 7.6

Opinion on Family Planning and Attitude Towards Medical Science

Opinion on Family Planning	Attitude towards medical science									Row Total
	Mohmora Village			Duhutimukh Village			Barpamua Village			
	Like	Dislike	Neutral	Like	Dislike	Neutral	Like	Dislike	Neutral	
Do not know	50 31.45 49.02	—	—	30 18.87 69.77	—	—	79 49.68 44.38	—	—	159 100.00
Do not get facilities	40 37.74 39.22	—	4 3.77 100.00	5 4.72 11.63	—	2 1.89 100.00	49 46.23 27.53	—	6 5.65 100.00	106 100.00
Do not like	12 17.14 11.76	—	—	8 11.53 18.60	—	—	50 71.43 28.09	—	—	70 100.00
Column Total	102 100.00		4 100.00	43 100.00		2 100.00	178 100.00		6 100.00	335 100.00

and high schools situated within or nearby the villages. In Mohmora village, there is one primary school with two Mishing teachers. About 88 students of the village are attending the primary school, 26 and more are in the high school. As informed by the villagers, now they have 4 graduates in their village. In Duhutimukh also, there is one L.P. school which was established as early as 1959. There are 60 students at L.P. school, 30 at high school and 4 at college. One post-graduate degree holder is also found in the village. In comparison to these two villages, Barpamua village is much bigger and its educational standard is higher to a certain extent. The number of students at L.P. school is more than 400, at high school it is more than 100, and at college the number of students is 20 or more. As informed by the villagers, there are 5 graduates, one post-graduate degree holder and one M.B.B.S. and several other diploma holders are there in the village. In fact, the above educational standard of the three villages is satisfactory as the total percentage of literacy of the Mishings was only 18.20 in 1971 (Census, 1971). In the L.P. school level, as informed by the respondents, almost all the village pupil use to go. But unfortunately the number of dropout students is larger than the continuity in going to school and further for higher qualification. Therefore, having so much students at the L.P. and H.E. school and colleges, the educational standard of the villages is a bit low. But it was found that most of the grown up generations are literate in comparison to the elder respondents of the present study. Having such a situation within the villages, most of the respondents are in favour of sending their children to schools and colleges for higher study. Table 7.7 shows the education of the respondents and the causes either for sending or not sending their children to school. The table indicates that out of 130 illiterate respondents 87 (66.92%) are sending their children to school, 28 (21.54%) are unable to send their children to school due to unsound economy and their children's engagement in agricultural activities. Secondly, out of 162 literate respondents 133 (82.09%) are sending their children to school, whereas 17 (10.49%) and 12 (7.42%) are unable to send due to unsound economic condition and engagement of their children in cultivation. Most surprisingly, out of 33 undermatric respondents 10 (30.31%) do not send their children to school due to other causes than that of unsound economy and engagement in agriculture.[3]

Though majority of the respondents do not send their children to school, they preferred various types of education either for their own sons

Table 7.7

Respondents' Qualification and Causes Either for Sending or not Sending Children to School

Educational qualification	Causes either for sending or not sending children to school				Row Total
	Sending children to school	Not, for unsound economy	Not, for engagement in cultivation	Not, for other reasons	
Illiterate	87 66.92 34.38	28 21.64 62.22	15 11.54 55.56	—	130 100.00
Literate	133 82.09 52.58	17 10.49 37.78	12 7.42 44.44	—	162 100.00
Undermatric	23 69.69 9.09	—	—	10 30.31 100.00	33 100.00
Matriculate and above	10 100.00 3.95	—	—	—	10 100.00
Column Total	253 100.00	45 100.00	27 100.00	10 100.00	335 100.00

and daughters or for their grandsons. According to the respondents, there is nothing wrong if they prefer education for their children even though some of them are unable to send their children to school. They said that personal attitude may be helpful to other children of the village. Therefore, they prefer both technical and non-technical education for their children. The table given below indicates the type of education preferred by the respondents for their children.

Table 7.8

Type of Education Preferred by the Respondents for Their Children

	Type of education	Total	percentage
1.	General	108	32.25
2.	Law	24	7.16
3.	Medicine	66	20.00
4.	Engineering	65	10.10
5.	No Choice	72	21.49
	Total	335	100.00

As the above table indicates, out of total respondents, 108 (32.25%) preferred general education for their children. The interest in law is not much among them. Only 24 (7.16%) respondents preferred it as the proposed future education of the sons and daughters. 66 (20.00%) respondents preferred medical education for their children and 65 (19.10%) respondents have given preference to engineering education. Combining both, this indicates the interest of the villagers in technical education. 72 (21.49%) respondents do not prefer any type of education for their children. These respondents have no choice of preference for their children, because, according to them, the merit of the children will lead them in their future course of education.

So far as the development of the entire Mishing community is concerned, the respondents have also given much stress on education. During the time of discussion in the field, most of the respondents told that acculturation and communication are more or less social processes which will come automatically in their society. But to apply the agents of changes properly, education is highly essential. And therefore, according to them, education is one of the main factors for the development of their society. That is why majority of the respondents preferred education as the first foremost criterion for development of their society. Table 7.9 indicates the result of the discussions.

Table 7.9

Attitude of the Respondents Towards Development and Preference Given by Them

Attitude	Preferences							Row Total
	1st	2nd	3rd	4th	5th	6th	7th	
Much acculturation is essential	2 0.59	5 1.49	27 8.05	37 11.04	73 21.79	49 14.62	142 42.42	335 100.00
Improved communication system	12 3.58	15 4.49	63 18.80	82 24.48	51 15.22	92 27.46	20 5.97	335 100.00
More agricultural production	52 15.52	127 37.49	63 18.30	39 11.64	42 12.53	7 2.08	5 1.49	335 100.00
Proper marketing centre	3 0.89	34 10.16	76 22.68	41 12.24	57 17.01	60 17.91	64 10.10	335 100.00
Proper education	269 80.31	26 7.76	24 7.16	12 3.58	4 1.19	—	—	335 100.00
Leaving social evils	1 0.29	50 14.93	55 16.42	57 17.01	79 23.58	77 22.98	16 4.78	335 100.00
Proper leadership	—	70 20.39	33 9.86	68 20.29	26 7.76	51 15.23	87 25.97	335 100.00

According to the aforementioned discussion, the table shows that 269 (80.31%) respondents have given first preference to education for the development of their community. All the respondents agreed that after having proper education they can eradicate the social evils. Therefore, out of the total respondents, only 1 (0.29%) respondents which is rather negligible, has given first preference in leaving of social evils for the development of their society. Next to education, the respondents have given stress on agricultural production. Therefore, for the second preference, 127 (37.94%) respondents have given their preference for more productions in agriculture. As indicated in the table, much acculturation for the development of the Mishings is preferred lastly. From the total respondents of 335, 14 (42.42%) preferred last preference for the necessity of much acculturation for the development of their society. From the table it is revealed that the people have given much interest in education and agricultural productions which will be responsible for the development of the whole Mishing community.

It was mentioned in the methodology chapter that after seeing the impact of the independent variables acculturation and communication on dependent variable development, the impact of marketing centres in and around the Mishing populated areas is attempted to be studied; because they are primarily responsible for the change of economy of the people which leads to the economic development of the people. From the economic point of view the marketing centres are important, specially in tribal areas (Sinha:1968), where economic forces cannot be ignored. Rostow (1960:2) says,

> Societies are interacting organisms. While it is true that economic change has political and social consequence, economic change is itself. . . the consequence of political and social as well as narrowly economic forces.

During the course of field study, it was found that in all the above consequences, marketing centres have been playing a significant role. The main centre for gathering is the daily and weekly marketing centres where people exchange their ideas through various socio-political gossips and economic exchanges. The daily and weekly markets at Jonai, weekly market at Bahir Jonai and few others serve the purpose for the people of the village Mohmora. They also frequently visit the urban places like Pashighat of Arunachal Pradesh and Silapathar, Dhemaji, Lakhimpur of Lakhimpur district. The main marketing centre of the villagers is Jonai. Similar facilities are enjoyed by the people of Duhutimukh village also.

The daily and weekly markets of Dhemaji, weekly marketing places like Jiadhol, Ghilamora and others are their marketing centres. The main marketing centre of the people is Dhemaji. The villagers of Barpamua have their marketing centres at Jengraimukh Tinali, Ratanpur, Phulani, Garmur, Kamalabari. They frequently visit urban places like Jorhat in the south bank of the Brahmaputra and Lakhimpur. The daily market place of Jengraimukh is the main marketing place of the villagers.

Now it is found that main marketing places for the three villages of this study are Jonai, Dhemaji and Jengraimukh Tinali. After a long period of observation and discussions, the result of impact of the marketing centres among the villagers of Mohmora, Duhutimukh and Barpamua are found as summarised below:

(1) The villagers, now-a-days, produce more agricultural products like paddy, mustard seeds, black pulse etc. to sell in the market. Interest in profit oriented agricultural production has been increasing due to facilities of market nearby the villages. The productions of domestic possessions are also increasing and the people of the villages have gradually been giving interest in making profit out of selling domestic possessions in the market.

(2) Petty businessmen like small shop-keepers and others are increasing in the market place of Jonai, Dhemaji and Jengraimukh Tinali some of which are being run by the villagers of Mohmora, Duhutimukh and Barpamua. It indicates the gradual emergence of entrepreneurship among the villages under study.

(3) As the people are now engaged in various businesses, the role of the middlemen (the Marwaris and other non-Mishing businessmen who often cheated the people few years back) is gradually decreasing. It was found in the field after participant observation that the people now-a-days directly sell their agricultural products and domestic possessions in the market. They neither believe nor depend upon the middleman who often tried to purchase the agricultural products and domestic possessions of the villagers.

(4) Investment of income according to need has been learnt by the villagers under study. According to them, it is mainly due to the impact of the nearby markets where they can come into contact with the non-tribal businessmen and learn to utilise their income.

From the above points it is clear that the economy of the people is gradually changing as they have the marketing facilities nearby their villages. The increase in businessmen, the replacement of middlemen, the learning of investment of income and the due importance given in more agricultural productions for profit making have been leading their development. It can be regarded as development because, as the villagers explained themselves, sound economy means the education, health and other overall improvement of their children and other members of the family; and that is why it can be regarded as their development. It was revealed in the field that the marketing centres in and around the Mishing villages have been contributing a major role for the development of the tribe.

After discussing the impact of acculturation and communication in the development of the Mishing community and with special reference to the marketing centres, it was found that the change in all aspects e.g., economy, education, health and others, is primarily the product of acculturation and communication. From the discussion of this chapter the findings can be summarised as follows :

(1) The socio-cultural change and change in polity, which is somehow or the other leading to the development of the people, is the product of acculturation and communication.

(2) The change of attitude towards economy, health and education is another major impact of acculturation and communication. Along with these two variables, marketing centres are playing cardinal role in the development of the people.

(3) And lastly, it is logical to argue that Hinduism is influencing in the socio-cultural change of the people and along with railways and marketing centres have been helping in the overall development of the villagers under study.

Apart from the above discussion, we can see the relative differential levels of development by explaining agricultural innovation, surplus production, educational development and possession of vehicle in the three villages under study.

(1) Table 7.10 indicates that the village Barpamua is much developed than the villages Mohmora and Duhutimukh. Since the stage of oral communication and the use of boats and elephants as the means of transportation, Barpamua village is better exposed to the outer world.

(2) The village Duhutimukh is having better transport communication. But the village is getting these facilities only from the mid sixties.

Table 7.10

Differential Levels of Development

Means	Villages						Rank		
	Village I Mohmora No. = 106		Village II Duhutimuph No. = 45		Village III Barpamua No. = 184		Village I	Village II	Village III
	Yes	No	Yes	No	Yes	No			
Agricultural innovation	36 33.96	70 66.04	15 33.33	30 66.66	64 34.78	120 65.22	II	III	I
Surplus Production	45 42.45	61 57.55	20 44.44	25 55.55	86 46.74	98 53.26	III	II	I
Educational Development	39 36.79	67 63.21	18 40.00	27 60.00	148 80.43	36 19.56	III	II	I
Possession of Vehicles	3 2.83	103 97.17	2 4.44	43 95.55	4 2.17	180 97.82	II	I	III

Contrary to it, Barpamua village is exposed to the main stream of cultural exchange and development as Majuli is a centre of cultural heritage of Assam.

(3) As indicated in the table, the village Barpamua ranks first in agricultural innovation, surplus production and in educational development. Therefore, Barpamua village is much developed than Mohmora and Duhutimukh villages.

It is to be noted in conclusion that the stage of development, as observed in the field, cannot be strictly regarded as the development of the tribe in the truest sense of the term. Here the gradual change of attitude in all aspects of life including economy, health, education and others are regarded as the development of the villagers, because the change in attitude will ultimately lead to their development.

References

1 Discussed specially in two of the investigators' papers namely', *Acculturation, Communication and Development in a Mishing Village*, in S. M. Dubey (ed.), North East India : A Sociological Study, 1978, Concept Publishing Company, Delhi and *Modernization of Economy and Occupation in a Mishing Village in Assam*, Published in North Eastern Research Bulletin, Vol. VIII, Summer 1979. The papers are based on two out of the three villages of the present study.

2 The table indicates the occupation of the respondents only. It does not necessarily indicate the total service holders, businessmen and others of the villages. It is to be noted here that the younger generation of the villages under study is rather much more engaged in service and business than the respondents of this study.

3 The respondents who do not send their children for education, though they are undermatric, have given causes for it. They said that they are unable to send their children to school in spite of so many attempts. According to them, the situation within the village itself is like that and therefore number of dropout children from school are higher. After the failure of the first attempt to educate their children, they give up the idea for the education of their children. Though the point seems to be weak, in fact, it is true, and such a situation was practically observed in the field work.

Aurora, G.S.
1974 Tribel, Caste, Class Encounters. Administrative. Staff College of India, Hyderabad.

Bhandari, J.S.
1974 Land and Social Structure : An Economic Study of a Mishing Village. In K.S. Mathur and B.C. Agrawal (eds.) Tribe, Caste and Peasantry. Ethnographic and Folk Culture Society, U.P., Lucknow.

Damle, Y.B.
1955 Communication of Modern Ideas and Knowledge in Indian Villages. Deccan College, Poona.

Dubey, S.M.
1978 Transportation of Tribal Communities in North-East India. Cyclostyled working paper, Panel II. The All India Sociological Conference, Jabalpur, Dec. 28-30, 1978.

Doley, D.
1973 The Socio-Economic Life of the Miri Tribe. North Eastern Research Bulletin, Vol. IV, Summer.

Hunter, W.W.
1879 A Statistical Account of Assam, Vol. II, Trubner and Co., London, Reprinted 1975 by B.R. Publishing Corporation, Delhi.

Puri, Rakshat
1972 Towards Security in the North East: Transportation and Nationalism. In K. Suresh Singh (ed.), Tribal Situation in India (Proceeding of a Seminar). Indian Institute of Advance Study, Simla

Rostow, W.W.
1960 The Stages of Economic Growth. Cambridge, Cambridge University Press.

Rao, Y.V. Lakshmana
1966 Communication and Development: A Study of Two Indian Villages. University of Minnesota Press, Minneapolis.

Srinivas, M.N.
1966 Social Change in Modern India. Berkeley and Los Angeles.

Sinha, D.P.
1968 Culture Change in an Inter-tribal Market. Asia Publishing House, Bombay.

Singh, K.S. (ed.)
1972 Tribal Situation in India (Proceeding of a Seminar). Indian Institute of Advance Study, Simla.

Vidyarthi, L.P. and B.K. Rai
1976 The Tribal Culture of India. The Concept Publishing Co., Delhi.

CHAPTER VIII

OVERVIEW AND CONCLUDING REMARKS

In the preceding chapter, we have discussed the process of acculturation, communication and development as visible among the Mishings. Apart from describing these processes, we have tried to examine into their relationship. The above processes have helped in the transformation of the Mishing social structure. Under the impact of these forces, now the Mishings are not 'isolates'. They have lost the basic features of the 'little community' (homogeneity, simplicity, self-sufficiency) as discussed by Redfield. The growing processes of interaction through Hinduism, Vaishnav religious institutions, Assamese language, communication networks and marketing centres have introduced them the features of 'peasantry'. On the one hand, they are the part of the peasant regional culture and on the other, they are linked with the main stream of the nation through commonly shared mythology, increasing polyglotism and growing inter-regional contacts through railways, markets and migration.

The North-East India is full of diversities as visible in tribes, languages and dialects, customs and traditions. The different communities are not at the equal level of material and non-material development. A few sociologists have tried to probe into the development of the tribes of this region by using the common models of social change in India, viz., sanskritization, westernization and development (Dubey: 1972a; 1976b; 1978d). It is found that the rate of literary and educational development is comparatively higher in those tribes who were converted to Christianity and less among those who profess Hinduism along with their tribal rituals (Dubey : 1972b). The later tribal groups, as stated by Ghurye (1963), are the worst sufferer of assimilational stresses and strains. In the context of these discussions, it can be said that the Mishings of Assam are in the second group who have been professing Hinduism along with their primitive customs and traditions. As shown by earlier studies (Doley : 1973; Bhandari: 1974; Sharma Thakur : 1976; Mipun: 1977), the process of development among the Mishings has been relatively mainly due to socio-cultural factors.

The main aim of discussion of the present study is on the following points:

(1) What is the impact of Hinduism in the process of acculturation of the Mishings? To what extent change has occurred in religion, food habits, language, housing pattern, dress and tools and implements of the Mishings?

(2) What is the nature, form and the impact of communication in general in the Mishing populated area?

(3) To what extent, acculturation and communication have influenced the socio-economic development of the Mishings?

I

The impact of Hinduism which is the main source of acculturation among the Mishings is found in all aspects of their life. In similar situation, Vidyarthi (1967) has tried to analyse the relationship between traditions of the dominant regional society and Hinduism. In the present context, the Hinduised Assamese peasantry is the dominant group in the Brahamputra Valley and the impact of its culture and traditions is visible among the Mishings.

It is found that the primitive religious practices of the Mishings have changed to a great extent. The resemblance of religious activities of the Mishings with their parent culture of Arunachal Pradesh is diminishing gradually. Due to the adoption of Hinduism as their religion, three distinct features are found among them. Firstly, their religion now-a-days is known as *Kewalia, Kalhanghati* or *Nisamalia* in place of the nameless animist belief and practices. Secondly, there is the emergence of *bhakats* and *hatulas* who replaced the importance of the tribal village priests known as *Miri* or *Mibu* in all religious activities; and thirdly, the introduction of *Namghar* as their religious institution which replaced the significance of *Murong* in their society. In spite of all these, a considerable number of respondents are found who are converted into *bhagavatia* or *mohapurushia* sects of Hinduism which means the further reformative attitude towards their present religion.

Formerly, the Mishings had no caste system and notion of purity and pollution in their food habits. This study reveals that after the conversion to Hinduism they gave up the habit of eating beef. Now-a-days, like the

Assamese Hindus, the villagers offer betelnut (*tamul-pan*) to the guests. The use of milk, oil, tea is gradually replacing the *apong* (rice beer) which is looked down by the people who are converted into Vaishnavism. It is found that next to their own dialect, the language of the Mishings is Assamese. Assamese is known to all respondents and Hindi and Bengali are also known to them to a certain extent. According to the respondents, the process of acculturation in the field of language among the *Samugurias* is so deep that they have forgotten their own Mishing dialect. The *mantras* used by the *bhakats*, *hatulas* are in Assamese language which shows the link between rituals and language. Moreover, though the traditional pattern of house-construction is common among the villagers, they often try to construct Assam type *pucca* buildings. Of course, it is still possible only among the economically sound and educated villagers. The various types of house-styles are found, i.e. the traditional *chung ghar*, Assam type *pucca* building, houses constructed on wooden platform, *kaccha mati ghar* etc. In regards to the clothes and dress, it is found that the indigenous practice of weaving is gradually declining. At present, excepting the women, the dress-pattern of the men is similar to that of the non-tribal Assamese. The traditional dresses are used only during the time of festivals and ceremonies. As regards the tools and implements, it is found that the agricultural tools and household utensils excepting few, are like the non-tribal Assamese.

In bringing about change in the Mishing social structure, the railway line and other means of communication networks have also played significant roles. A few studies have thrown light on the role of communication networks in social change (Atal : 1977; Kiernan: 1977). The introduction of the railway line in the Mishing areas has brought about considerable change. It is playing its role mainly in three areas, first of all, it has increased horizon of social intercourse of the villagers with other non-tribal people which has led to the change in their social, economic and political life. Secondly, it has augmented immigration. The contact with migrants has made Mishing villagers polyglot. Thirdly, as the journey fare in train is cheap, it helps in minimising their expenditure. More or less the similar role is being played by the road transportation. The marketing centres have also helped in developing interaction among the people. A few villagers are found to subscribe newspaper and owning radio-sets. There is two-fold impact on the villagers, firstly, in the evening gatherings, where the literates and students read out the news, the villagers have the chance to know about the happenings. Secondly, they have the opportunity to sort out their problems because of the growing political consciousness and awareness. The radio is used primarily for recreation. It is found in the study that bi-cycle is regarded as one of the most important possessions. It is one of the most important means to carry their agricultural products to the markets and means of transportation to visit their relatives.

Several studies (Mukhopadhyaya : 1967; Sinha : 1968) have tried to analyse the roles of marketing centres in socio-economic change in tribal areas. The economic development of the tribes mainly rests on the growing up of marketing centres around the villages. As mentioned earlier, the marketing centres have accelerated the process of economic and cultural exchange. The Mishing villagers sell their agricultural products in these centres. The demands of marketing centres have commercialised the agricultural products and there is growing trend to produce cash crops. The influence of the middlemen, due to whom the villagers formerly lost the actual price of their products, is declining because of the marketing facilities available nearby the villagers.

II

Various studies on the socio-cultural change among the castes and tribes of India have been conducted earlier to the present study. There are several theoretical and contextual aspects of present study, i.e., the question of caste-tribe relationship, sanskritisation and tribe-folk, peasant and urban continuum.

At first let us try to examine into the question of caste-tribe relationship (Baily : 1961; Dumont : 1962; Volchok : 1964; Oran : 1965; Reddy: 1973) and sanskritization (Srinivas : 1966). An analysis of the process of acculturation among the Mishings clearly indicates the trends of sanskritisation through the introduction of Hindu beliefs, myths, legends, religious ideology, and institutions and notion of purity and pollution related with food and social interaction. The studies of the Oran (Singh : 1964), the Santhals (Oran : 1965) and the Nilgiri hill dwellers (Gould : 1967) have tried to examine into the impact of Hinduism, great traditions and *Jajmani* relationships on the tribes. After the adoption of Hinduism, almost the similar trends are visible among the Mishings also. In many parts of Upper Assam, the Mishings are living alongwith other Hindu castes in multicaste villages, some of them have lost their compact territories, and have forgotten their dialects. In the Hindu hierarchy, their position is low but constitutionally in all parts of Assam and socially and culturally in Dhemaji and Jonai sub-divisions of Lakhimpur district, they have preserved some of the basic features of tribal structure; i.e., compact territory, dialect and culture. As regards the question of the tribe-folk, peasant and urban continuum (Redfield : 1953a, 1955b), the trends of folk and peasantry and the influences of urban centres are already visible among the Mishings. Keeping in view the works of Srinivas and Redfield, Aurora (1972) has studied socio-cultural change among the Bhilalas of Alirajpur where he has given special stress on folk-urban continuum.

The Mishings have tried to adjust tribal institutions and practices with the growing impact of Hinduism. The Christian tribes of the North-East India have almost abandoned their tribal customs, practices and institutions, but the tribes who are converted into Hinduism are still practising their tribal rituals along with Hinduism. The best example is the Mishings of the present study. Few of the examples are quoted here. The *bihu* festival in Assam i.e. *rangali bihu, Kati bihu* and *Bhugali bihu* are performed by the Mishings with equal enthusiasm as they are celebrated by other Assamese. The festival is accepted as part and parcel of their life. But they perform it according to their own traditional way. Similarly, their *sraddha* ceremony is almost similar to that of the non-tribal Assamese. But the ritual activities are done according to their traditional practices. That is applicable in all other aspects of their life which are accepted from non-tribal Assamese and to whom we often regard as acculturation.

III

It is mentioned in the introductory chapter that no proper studies have been done on the Mishings regarding their cultural change and development. Only Doley (1973) and Bhandari (1974) raised some of the issues regarding the backwardness of the Mishings. According to them, the main reason behind the backwardness is cultural factor. The development of the Mishings, according to them, is arrested mainly due to some of the tribal practices which encourage wastage. After proper scrutiny of the findings of the present study, the following issues seem to be seriously influencing the Mishings:

It is found that two distinct groups opposing each other have emerged among them. The first group which is composed of illiterates and elders, try to retain their traditional practices, norms and institutes, whereas the second group composed of educated and youngers is more prone to modern ideas and values (Chandra: 1964; Singh : 1970).

Due to the process of acculturation, some of the traditional practices and institutions are abandoned among the Mishings. For instance, the functions and position of the *mibu* are being replaced by *bhakats* and *hatulas*. Similarly, the place of *murong* is replaced by *namghar*. So, a gradual process of detribalisation is visible among them.

The process of acculturation and growing communication have linked Mishings with regional culture and the national main stream. But really several new issues have emerged among them. Now, a group of educated Mishings are showing concern for the growth of their dialect, preservation of their music, songs and dance and the distinct identity. A section of them have demanded the use of the Roman-script for their dialect. It may not be regarded as a counter-process of acculturation but these new trends are also visible among them.

The process of development, agricultural innovations, impact of marketing centres have widened the gulf between the rich and the poor among the Mishings. The new educational facilities, reservation of jobs and politics have created new elite among them. These processes require separate and detailed studied.

References

1. The religion of the Adis, Nishis and others of the former Abor group of Arunachal Pradesh can be regarded as the parent culture of the Mishings as they migrated mainly from Siang district of Arunachal. The resemblance between the culture of the Adis and Mishings was very much there few years back. Now due to the much more impact of the Assamese culture, the Mishings are gradually changing and the similarities are weakening gradually. From sociological point of view, this can be said that the parent cultures for the Mishings are both the Adis culture and the non-tribal Assamese culture. Amidst the both they are changing gradually. (The impact of the parent culture is discussed elaborately in Zillur Khan's Study Cultural Fusion : A case study of St. Martir Island in the Bay of Bengal, 1968. Man in India, Vol. 48, Oct.-Dec.)

Aurora, G.S.

1972 Tribe-Caste-Class Encounters, Administrative Staff College of India, Hyderabad.

Atal, Yogesh.

1977 Communication and Nation Building in India. In M.N. Srinivas and others (eds.), Dimensions of Social Change in India, Allied Publishers Pvt. Ltd., Bombay.

Baily, F.G.

1961 Tribe and Caste in India. Contributions to Indian Sociology, Vol. V.

Bhandari, J.S.

1974 Land and Social Structure: An Economic Study of a Mishing Village. In K.S. Mathur and B.C. Agrawal (eds.), Tribe, Caste and Peasantry. Ethnographic and Folk-Culture Society, U.P., Lucknow.

Chandra, Prabhat

1964 Communication of Some New Ideas in a Madhya Pradesh Village : A sociological study conducted in a mixed village. The Eastern Anthropologist 3, Vol. XVII, Sept.-Dec.

Dumont, L.

1962 Tribe and Caste in India, Correspondents, Contributions to Indian ·Sociology, Vol. VI.

Dubey, S.M.

1972a Tradition, Transition and Change in Assamese Society. In N.H. Hazarika and others (eds.), Silver Jubilee Commemoration Volume, Sibsagar College, Joysagar.

1972b Education, Social Changes and Political Consciousness Among the Tribes of the North-East India. In K. Suresh Singh (ed.), Tribal Situation in India (Proceedings of a Seminar), Indian Institute of Advance Study, Simla.

1972c Modernization among the Tribes of North-Eastern India (Assam). In S.K. Srivastava (ed.), Tradition and Modernization, Indian International Publications, P.B. 79, Katra Road, Allahabad.

1972d Transformation in Tribal Communities in North-East India, Working Paper, The All India Sociological Conference, Jabalpur, Dec. 28-30, 1978.

Doley, D.

1973 The Socio-economic Life of the Miri tribe. North-Eastern Research Bulletin, Vol. IV, Summer.

Ghurye, G.S.

1963 The Scheduled Tribes, Popular Prakashan, Bombay 4.

Gould, Harold A.

1967 Priest and Counterpart : A Structural Analysis of *Jajmani* Relationship in the Hindu plains and the Nilgiri Hills.Contributions to Indian Sociology, No. 1 (New Series).

Kiernan, J.P.

1977 Public Transport and Private Risk : Zionism and the Black Commuter in South Africa. Journal of Anthropological Research 2 Vol. 33. Summer.

Mukhopadhyaya, T.

1967 Ecology and Markets in Eastern Midnapur, Man in India, Vol. 47, Jan.-March.

Mipun, J.

1977 Acculturation, Communication and Development in a Mishing Village. In S.M. Dubey (ed.), North-East India. A Sociological Study. Concept Publishing Company, 65 E. Anand Nagar, Delhi.

Oran, Martin

1965 The Santhal : A Tribe in Search of a Great Tradition. Wayne State Universities Press, Detroit.

Redfield, R.

1953a Primitive World and its Transformations. Cornell University Press, New York.

1955b Peasant Society and Culture, Chicago.

Reddy, N.S.
1973 Caste in a Tribal Society, the Formative Process. Contributions to Indian Sociology, No. VII.

Srinivas, M.N.
1966 Social Change in Modern India. California University Press.

Sinha, D.P.
1968 Culture Change in An Inter-tribal Market, Asia Publishing House, Bombay.

Singh, P.N.
1964 Sources of Hindu Influences on Oraons Living in Purnea District. Journal of Social Research, 7, Nos. 1 & 2

Sharma Thakur, G.C.
1976 Socio-economic Change in Post-independence Period in a Tribal Village in Assam. The North-Eastern Research Bulletin, Vol. VII., Summer.

Vidyarthi. L.P.
1967 Social Duplication of Industrialisation in Tribal Bihar. The Anthropologist, Special Vol. II.

APPENDICES

APPENDIX I

BIBLIOGRAPHY

(a) Books/Articles

(I) General

Aiyer, A.J. and others
1955 Studies in Communication, London, Secker & Warburg.

Aron, Raymond
1967 The Industrial Society. New York: Praeger.

Aurora, G.S.
1972 Tribe-Caste-Class Encounters. Administrative Staff College of India, Hyderabad.

Atal, Yogesh
1977 Communication and Nation-building in India. In M.N. Srinivas and others (eds.), Dimensions of Social Change in India. Allied Publishers Pvt. Ltd.

Bacon, W.R. and M.J. Herskovitz (eds.)
1959 Continuity and Change in African Culture.

Broadbent, D.E.
1958 Perception and Communication, New York : Pergamon.

Bhattacharya, V.R.
1976 Communication in a Global Village, Chetana Publications, New Delhi.

Barringer, H.R., G.I. Blankston and R.W. Mark

1965 Social Change in Developing Areas. Cambridge, Harsachustta : Schenkman Publishing Company.

Boulding, Kenneth, E.

1963 The Image. Ann Arbor: University of Michigan Press.

Crowly. Thomas H.

1962 Modern Communication. New York : Columbia University Press.

Chaterji, S.K.

1951 Kirata-Jana Krti - The Indo-Mongoloids - Their Contribution to the History and Culture of India. Based upon Pratibha Devi Lectures, delivered at Jorhat, Assam in 1947. Published in 1951 by the Asiatic Society, 1 Park Street, Calcutta-16.

Damle, Y.B.

1955 Communication and Modern Ideas and Knowledge in Indian Villages. Deccan College. Poona.

Dexter, L.A.

1964 People Society and Mass Communication. New York: Free Press.

Dube, S.C.

1967 A Note on Communication, Innovation and Planned Change in India. In Daniel Lerner and W. Schramm (eds.), Communication and change in Developing Countries. East West Centre, Honolulu.

1977 The Tribal Heritage of India (ed.), Vol. I : Ethnicity, Identity and Interaction. Vikas Publishing House Pvt. Ltd., New Delhi.

Dutta Majumder, N.

1956 The Santhal. Calcutta: Anthropological Survey of India.

Eisenstadt, S.N.

1961 Essay on the Sociological Aspects of Political and Economic Development. The Hague, Monton.

Eberts P.R. and Frank, W. Young

1971 Sociological Variables of Development : Their Range and Characteristics, In G.M. Beal, R.C. Powers and

E.W. Coward Jr. (Eds.), Sociological Perspectives of Domestic Development. Ames : Iowa State University Press.

Friedle, John

1976 Cultural Anthropology, Harper's College Press. A Department of Harper and Row Publications, New York.

Gould J. and W.L. Kolb

1964 A Dictionary of Social Sciences. The Free Press.

Greiger, H. Kent

1971 Societal Development : Notes on the Vestment of a Concept. In G.M. Beal, R.C. Powers and E.W. Coward Jr. (eds.), Sociological Perspectives of Domestic Development. Ames : Iowa State University Press.

Ghurye, G.S.

1940 Caste and Class in India. Bombay: Popular Book Depot.

1943 The Aborigins - So-called and Their Future. Institutes of Politics and Economics, Poona.

1963 The Scheduled Tribes. Popular Prakashan, Bombay.

Goode, W.J. and P.K. Hatt

1952 Method in Social Research. McGraw Hill Kogakusha Ltd., Tokyo.

Gorer, Geoffrey.

1938 Himalayan Villages : An Account of Lepchas of Sikkim (with an introduction by J.H. Hutton). London : Michael, Josheph.

Herskovitz, M.J.

1938 Acculturation : The Study of Culture Contact. New York: J.J. Augustin.

1955 Cultural Anthropology : An Abridged Revision of Man . and His Work). Oxford and I.B. Publishing Co., Delhi.

Hollowell, A.I.

1957 Socio-psychological Aspects of Acculturation. In R. Linton (ed.), The Science of Man in the World Crisis. New York: Columbia University Press.

Hochings, Poul
1977 Communication Networks. In M.N. Srinivas and others (eds.), Dimensions of Social Change in India. Allied Publishers Pvt. Ltd., Bombay.

Horowits, I.L.
1966 Three Worlds of Development. In G.M. Beal, R.C. Powers and E.W. Coward Jr. (eds.), Sociological Perspectives of Domestic Development. Ames : Iowa University Press.

Hobbs, D.J.
1971 Some Contemporary Sociological Perspectives Regarding Social Change. In Ibid.

Hoselitz, B.P.
1960 Sociological Aspects of Economic Growth. New York:. The Free Press of Glence.

Inkeles, Alex
1966 Modernization of Man. In M. Weiner (ed.), Modernization. New York: Basic Books.

Jay, Edward
1961 Revitalization Movement in Tribal India. In L.P. Vidyarthi (ed.), Aspects of Religion in Indian Society. Meerut: Kedar Nath Ram Nath.

Kahl, Joseph A.
1968 The Measurement of Modernization. Austin : University of Texas Press.

Kulkarni, M.G.
1974 Problems of Tribal Development : A case study. Parimal Prakashan.

Karve, Iravati
1942 Some Studies in the Making of a Culture Pattern. In J.R. Mills and others (ed.), Essays in Anthropology, presented to Rai Bahadur S.C. Roy. Lucknow: Maxwell & Co.

Lundberg, G.A. C.C. Shrag and O.N. Lerren
1954 Sociology. New York: Harper and Brothers.

Linton, Ralph

1940 Acculturation in Seven American Indian Tribes.

Lerner, Daniel

1958 The Passing of Traditional Society. New York: Free Press.

Moore, W.E.

1965 Social Change. Prentice Hall of India (Pvt.) Ltd. New Delhi.

Mead, Margaret

1932 The Changing Culture of an Indian Tribe. New York: Columbia University Press.

Majumder, D.N.

1937 A Tribe in Transition. A Study in Culture Patterns. London: Longman Green & Co.

Myrdal, G.

1968 Asian Drama. Penguin Books, U.K.

Martindale, Don

1962 Social Change and Cultural Change. Princeton New Jersey : D. Van Nostrand.

McClelland, David C.

1961 The Achieving Society. Princeton, New Jersey : D. Van Nostrand.

Murdock, G.P.

1955 On the Definition of Acculturation. In H.P. Fairchild (ed.), Dictionary of Sociology. Ames Iowa : Littlefield; Adams.

Malinowski, Bronislow

1945 The Dynamics of Culture Change : An Enquiry into the Race Relations in Africa. New Haven : Yale University Press.

Mehta, N.B.

1927 Indian Railways : Rates and Regulations. P.S. King and Sons Ltd., London.

Newmen, John B.

1966 A Rationale for a Definition of Communication. In Alfed G. Smith (ed.), Communication and Culture. Holt, Rinehart and Winston, New York.

Oran, Martin.

1965 The Santal : A Tribe in Search of a Great Tradition. Wayne State Universities Press, Detroit.

Powell, J.W.

1880 Introduction to the Study of Indian Languages. Washington D.C.: Government Printing Office.

Prasad, A.

1960 Indian Railways. Asia Publishing House, Bombay.

Quine, Willard Van Orman

1960 Ward and Object. Cambridge Mass : The MIT Press, New York, Wiley.

Redfield, Robert

1953 The Primitive World and its Transformation. Ithaca, New York: Cornell University Press.

Rowstow, W.W.

1960 The Stages of Economic Growth. Cambridge: Cambridge University Press.

Rao, Y.V. Laksmana

1966 Communication and Development : A Study of Two Indian Villages. University of Minnesota Press, Minneapolis.

Smelser, Neli J.

1963 Mechanism of Change and Adjustment to Change. In B.E. Hoselitz and W.E. Moore (eds.), Industrialization and Society, Paris - the Hague : UNESCO, Monton.

Srinivas, M.N.

1942 Marriage and Family in Mysore. Bombay.

1966 Social Change in Modern India. Berkeley and Los Angeles.

Sinha, D.P.

1968 Cultural Change in an Intertribal Market. Asia Publishing House, Bombay.

Sachchidanand

1964 Cultural Change in Tribal Bihar. Calcutta: Bookland Pvt. Ltd.

Schramm, W.

1964 Mass Media and National Development : The Role of Information in Developing Countries. Stanford University Press, Stanford.

Spindler, G.D.

1955 Socio-cultural and Psychological Process in Minomini Acculturation. Berkeley : University of California Press.

Selltiz, C.M., M. Johoda and others (eds.)

1965 Research Methods in Social Relations. Methuen & Co. Ltd., 11 New Fetter Lane, E.C. 4.

Sengupta, S.K.

1966 Assimilation of Cultural Traits by the Mahlis of Midnapur. Calcutta: Calcutta University.

Saxena, K.K.

1962 Indian Railways : Problems and Prospects. Vora & Co. Publishers Pvt. Ltd., Bombay-2.

Singh, K.S. (ed.)

1972 Tribal Situation in India (Proceeding of a Seminar). Indian Institute of Advance Study, Simla.

Vidyarthi, L.P. and B.K. Rai

1976 The Tribal Culture of India. The Concept Publishing Co., Delhi.

Vidyarthi L.P.

1978 Rise of Anthropology in India. Vol. I, Concept Publishing Co., Delhi.

Wilson, Godray and Monicatt Wilson

1965 The Analysis of Social Change : Based on Observations in Central Africa. Cambridge University Press.

Warner, W. Keith

1971 Structural Matrix of Development. In G.M. Beal, R.C. Powers and R.W. Coward Jr. (eds.), Sociological Perspective of Development. Ames: Iowa State University Press.

Weber, Max

1958 The Protestant Ethic and the Spirit of Capitalism. T. Parsons (Trans), New York : Scrubner's and Sons.

Warshay, Leon H.

1964 Breath of Perspective and Social Change. In G.K. Zollschan and W. Hirsch (eds.) Exploration in social Change. Boston : Houghton Mifflin.

(II) Books/Articles on Assam, North-East India

Baines, Sir A.

1912 Ethnography (Castes and Tribes). Concept Publishing Co., Delhi.

Bhandari, J.S.

1974 Land and Social Structure : An Economic Study of a Mishing Village. In K.S. Mathur and B.C. Agrawal (eds.), Tribe, Caste and Peasantry. Ethnographic and Folk Culture Society, U.P., Lucknow.

Boruah, B.K.

1951 A Cultural History of Assam (early period). Lawyer's Book Stall, Gauhati, Assam.

Dubey, S.M.

1972 Education, Social Change and Political Consciousness Among the Tribes of North-East India. In K.S. Singh (ed.), Tribal Situation in India. Indian Institute of Advanced Study, Simla.

1972 Tradition, Transition and Change in Assamese Society. In N.H. Hazarika and others (eds.), Silver Jubilee Commemoration Volume, Sibsagar College, Joysagar.

1976 Modernization Among the Tribes of North Eastern India (Assam). In S.K. Srivastava (ed.), Tradition and Modernization. Indian International Publications, Allahabad.

1977 Modernization in Arunachal Pradesh. Census Publications, Delhi.

1977 North-East India : A Sociological Study. Concept Publishing Co., Delhi.

1978 Transformation in Tribal Communities in North East India. Working Paper, The All India Sociology Conference, Jabalpur, Dec. 28-30, 1978.

Das, B.M.

1967 Assamese Culture and the Hill People of North-East India. In R. Mitra and B. Das Gupta (eds.), A Common Perspective for North-East India, Calcutta: Pannalal Das Gupta.

Devi, Lakshmi

1968 The Socio-Economic Life of the Miri Tribe. North-Eastern Research Bulletin, Vol. IV, Summer.

Endle, S.

1911 The Kachari. Reprinted 1975 by Cosmo Publications, Delhi.

Elwin, Verrier

1964 A Philosophy for NEFA, Shillong.

Furer-Haimendorf, Christoph Von

1939 The Naked Nagas. London : Routledge and Kegan Paul.

1962 The Apa-Tanis and Their Neighbourhood. London: Routledge and Kegan Paul.

Goswami, B.B.

1972 The Tribes of Assam : Few Comments on their Social and Cultural Ties with the Non-Tribes. In K.S. Singh (ed.), Tribal Situation in India (Proceeding of a Seminar), Indian Institute of Advanced Study, Simla.

Gait, Sir Edward

1905 A History of Assam. Thacker Spink & Co. (1933) Pvt. Ltd. (Reprinted in 1967).

Hunter, W.W.

1979 A Statistical Account of Assam. Vol. II, Trubner & Co., London. Reprinted 1975 by B.R. Publishing Corporation, Delhi.

Hutton, J.H.

1921 The Angami Nagas. London : Macmillan.

Michell, John F.

1883 The North-East Frontier of India (A Topographical, Political and Military Report). Reprinted 1973 by Vivek Publishing House, Delhi.

M' Cosh, John.

1937 Topography of Assam. Reprintd 1975 by Sanskaran Prakashak, Delhi.

Majumder, D.N.

1967 Social Organization of the Koch of Garo Hills. In R. Mitra and B. Das Gupta (eds.), A Common Perspective of North-East India. Calcutta : Pannalal Das Gupta.

1972 A Study of Tribe-Caste Continuum and the Process of Sanskritization among the Bodo-speaking Tribes of the Garo Hills. In K.S. Singh (ed.), Tribal Situation in India. Indian Institute of Advance Study, Simla.

1972 Acculturation among the Hajong of Meghalaya. Man in India I, Vol. 52. Jan-March.

Mipun, J.

1976 Acculturation, Communication and Development among the Dimasa Kacharis of the North Cachar Hills District in Assam. North Eastern Research Bulletin, Vol. VII, Summer.

1977 Acculturation, Communication and Development in a Mishing Village. In S.M. Dubey (ed.), North-East India: A Sociological Study. Concept Publishing Co., Delhi.

Pegu, N.S.

1956 The Miris or the Mishings of the Brahamaputra Valley, Kumarbari, Majuli, Assam.

1981 The Mishings of the Brahamaputra Valley, Dibrugarh, Assam.

Puri, Rakshat

1972 Towards Security in the North-East : Transportation and Nationalism. In K.S. Singh (ed.), Tribal Situation in India (Proceeding of a Seminar). Indian Institute of Advance Study, Simla.

Robinson, W.

1941 A Descriptive Account of Assam. Reprinted 1975 by Sanskaran Prakashak, Delhi.

Roy, Sachin.

1966 Aspects of Padam Minyong Culture. NEFA, Shillong.

Roy Burman, B.K. and S.P. Thakral

1970 Demographic and Socio-economic Profiles of the Hill Areas of North-East India. Census of India 1961, New Delhi : Office of the Registrar General, India.

Sinha, Raghubir

1962 The Akas. Shillong : Research Department, Advisers Secretariat.

Sharma Thakur, G.C.

1976 Socio-Economic Change in post-Independence Period in a Tribal Village in Assam. The North-Eastern Research Bulletin, Vol. III, Summer.

Wadell, L.A.

1901 The Tribes of the Brahmaputra Valley. Reprinted 1975 by Sanskaran Prakashak, Delhi.

(b) Books/Articles in Assamese

Loying, T.

1972 Mishing Bhasa Nukua Mishing. In B. Kagyung (ed.), Mishing Sanskritir Alekhya, 1972, Birubari, Gauhati.

Narzi, Bhaben

1966 Boro-Kachari Samaj aur Sanskriti. Lawyers Book Stall, Gauhati.

Payengkataki, S.

1935 Miri Jatir Buranji. Mornoi Bebejia, Dhemaji.

Pegu, N.C.

1972 Miri ba Mishing. In B. Kagyung (ed.), Mishing Sanskritir Alekhya, Birubari, Guwahati.

Pamegam, Tarun Chandra.

1972 Miri ba Mishing. In ibid.

Padun, N.

1972 Mishing Janajatir Parishay. In ibid.

1972 Mishing Sakalar Baibahik Niti, ibid.

1972 Mishing Bhasa. ibid.

1972 Mishing Loka Sahitya, ibid.

Regon, D.

1972 Mishing Bibah Paddhati. ibid.

(c) Journals

Alba, Richard D.

1976 Social Assimilation among American Catholic National Origin Groups. American Sociological Review 6. Vol. 41.

Agrawal, B.C.

1968 From Commerce to Conquest : A Historical Study of Acculturation in India. The Eastern Anthropologist 1. Vol. XXI, Jan.-April.

Beals, Ralph L.

1951 Urbanism, Urbanization and Acculturation. American Anthropologist. New Series 53 : 1-10.

Bhumer, Herbert

1966 The Idea of Social Development. Studies in Comparative International Development 2 : 3-11.

Bebechuk, Nicholas

1962 The Role of the Research as Participant Observer and Participant-as-Observer in the Field Situation. Human Organization 3, Vol. 21.

Bruyn, Severyn

1963 Methodology of Participant Observation. Human Organization 3, Vol. 22.

Baily, F.G.

1961 Tribe and Caste in India. Contributions to Indian Sociology, Vol. V.

Chattopadhyay, K.P.

1922 An Essay on the History of Mewar Culture. Journal of Proceeding of Asiatic Society of Bengal (New Series), No. 3, Vol. XXIII.

1949 The Tribal Problem and its Solution. The Eastern Anthropologist 1, Vol. III, Sept.

Chandra, Prabhat

1964 Communication of Some New Ideas in a Madhya Pradesh Village. The Eastern Anthropologist 3, Vol. XVII, Sept.-Dec.

Dube, S.C.

1949 Some Aspects of Tribal Problems. The Eastern Anthropologist 1, Vol. III, Sept.

Dumont, L.

1962 Tribe and Caste in India. Correspondents. Contributions to Indian Sociology, Vol. VI.

Eaton, Joseph W.

1952 Controlled Acculturation : A Survival Technique of the Hutterites. American Sociological Review 17 : 331-340.

Elselein, E.B. and M. Topper

1976 Media Anthropology, A Theoretical Framework. Human Organization 2, Vol. 5, Summer.

Ghurye, G.S.

1952 Social Change in Maharashtra. Part I, Sociological Bulletin 1, Vol. VI.

Gould, Harold A.

1967 Priest and Counterpart : A Structural Analysis of Jajmani Relationship in the Hindu Plains and the Nilgiri Hills. Contributions to Indian Sociology. No. 1 (New Series).

Keesing, F.M.

1954 Acculturation : An Exploratory Formulation. American Anthropologist, Vol. 54.

Kim, Kyong-Dong

1973 Towards a Sociological Theory of Developments : A Structural Perspective. Rural Sociology 4, Vol. 38, Winter.

Kiernan, J.P.

1977 Public Transport and Private Risk : Zionism and the Black Commuter in South Africa. Journal of Anthropological Research 2, Vol. 33, Summer.

Khan, Zillur

1968 Cultural Fusion : A Case Study of St. Martir Island in Bay of Bengal. Man in India, Vol. 48, Oct.-Dec.

Lewis, Russell, E.
1970 Controlled Acculturation Revisited : An Examination of Differential Acculturation and Assimilation between the Hutterian Brethren and the Old Order Amish. International Review of Modern Sociology 1, Vol. 6, Spring.

Lionberger, Herbert F. and B.A. Heddy
1976 Reference Group Influence on Extension Communication of Social Science Faculty. Rural Sociology, Vol. 41, Spring.

Moore, W.E.
1960 A Reconsideration of Theory of Social Change. American Sociological Review 6, Vol. 25, Dec.

McGee, W.J.
1960 Piratical Acculturation. American Anthropologist, Selected Papers from the American Anthropologist, 1888-1920. Evanston III Row Peterson (First Published in Vol. II of the American Anthropologist, New Series).

Mishra, V.M.
1973 The Communication Media and Learning for Modernization : A Conceptual Model. Indian Journal of Social Research 2, Vol. XIV, August.

Mehra, J.D.
1954 The Naiks of Ramgarh and the Effects of Acculturation on Them. The Anthropologist 1, Vol. I, August.

Majumder, D.N.
1949 The Changing Canvas of Tribal Life. Eastern Anthropologist 3, Vol. I.

Mukhopadhyaya, T.
1967 Ecology and Markets in Eastern Midnapur. Man in India 1, Vol. 47, Jan.-March.

Newcomb, W.W.
1956 The Culture and Acculturation of the Dalware Indians.

Parsons, Talcott
1961 Some Considerations on the Theory of Social Change. Rural Sociology 26, Sept.

Redfield, R. R. Linton and M.J. Herskovitz

1936 Memorandum on the Study of Acculturation. American Anthropologist 38, pp. 149-52.

Redfield, Robert

1955 The Social Organization of Tradition. Far Eastern Quarterly, Vol. 15, pp. 13-21.

Reddy, N.S.

1973 Caste in a Tribal Society, the Formative Process. Contributions to Indian Sociology, No. VII.

Sharp, Lauriston

1952 Steel Axes for Stone-age Australians. Human Organization 11 : 17-22.

Seers, D.

1970 The Meaning of Development. The Agricultural Development Council Reprint (Sept.).

Srinivas, M.S.

1961 Dominant Caste in Rampura. American Anthropologist 1, Vol. 61.

Sinha, D.P.

1963 The Role of Paharia in Tribal Acculturation in a Central Indian Market. Ethnology 2, Vol. II.

Sahay, K.N.

1962 Trends of Sanskritization among the Oraons. Bulletin of Bihar Tribal Research Institute-2, Vol. IV.

Sinha, Surajit

1962 State Formation and Rajput Myth in Central India. Man in India 2, Vol. 42.

Srivastava, S.K.

1949 Some Problems of Culture Contacts among the Tharus. Eastern Anthropologist 1, Vol. III.

Singh, P.N.

1964 Sources of Hindu Influences on Oraon Living in Purnea District, Journal of Social Research 1&2, Vol. VII.

Taske, Raymond H.C. Jr. and B.H. Nelson

1974 Acculturation and Assimilation : A Clarification. American Ethnology 1 : 351-367.

Von Wiese, L.

1956 The Sociological Study of Social Change. Transactions of the Third World Congress of Sociology 1 : 1-9.

Vidyarthi, L.P.

1967 Social Duplication of Industrialisation in Tribal Bihar. The Anthropologist, Special Vol. II.

(d) Govt. Records etc.

1. Census of India, Assam State, 1971, Part V : Social Tables, Ethnographic Notes on Scheduled Castes and Scheduled Tribes.
2. Statistical Handbook of Assam, 1976.
3. Statistical Handbook of Assam, 1971.
4. Note Book of Survey and Construction Organization of N.F. Railway, Maligaon, Guwahati.

APPENDIX II

(a) VILLAGE SCHEDULE

(SCHEDULE I)

Acculturation, Communication and Development among the Mishings (Miris) in Assam

Investigator	*Supervisor*
Sri Jatin Mipun, M.A.	Dr. S.M..Dubey, M.A., Ph.D.
Research Scholar,	Prof. & Head of Sociology Deptt.,
Dibrugarh University.	Dibrugarh University.

A. General Description of the Village

1. Name of the Village :
2. Location : District/Sub-division/block/gaon panchayat
3. Total households
4. Total population : Male/female

B. Acculturation

Religion

1. Number of *pujas* and festivals practised by the people. Traditional story of origin/oaths and ordeals/pregnancy/child birth and name giving ceremony/marriage/disposal of dead /priesthood etc.
2. Religious institutions.
3. Attitudes towards the maintenance of purity.
4. Changes in religious practice.
5. Sources of influence of the neighbouring Hindus.

Food Habit

1. Main diet of the people.
2. No. of daily meal.
3. Nature of diet related to the religious performance.
4. Habit in using flesh, milk, fish, egg, oil as their diet.
5. Importance of rice beer among the people.

Language

1. Language of the people.
2. Other languages known by the people : Assamese/English/ Hindi/Bengali.
3. Sources for knowing these languages : Communication/marketing centres/education/medium of instruction/students/leaders.

House

1. Housing pattern.
2. Attitude towards the traditional housing pattern.
3. Room for sleep/kitchen/household goods/guests etc.
4. Type of construction of the youth club, religious institution.
5. No. of modern type (pucca) houses in the village. Sources for the construction - sound economic condition/education/influence of the neighbouring non-tribal people/changes in attitude.

Dress

1. Dress pattern of the men and women.
2. Any typical dress in festival/religious performances.
3. Dresses are generally of own production/machinemade.
4. Attitude towards the machinemade cloth.

Tools & Implements

1. Number and name of the tools and implements used in household activities/agriculture/fishing.
2. Tools are of their own production/machine-made.
3. Attitude towards the machine-made tools and implements.

Clan Organization/Kinship Terminology/Inheritance among the People

Elements of Hindu Customs that are found among the People

C. Communication

1. Number of roads connected with the village : Motorable/non-motorable.
2. Distance from the railway station/ferryghat.
3. Number of marketing centres confined to the village.
4. Post and telegraph office.
5. Number of radio/transistor/newspapers/magazine in the village.
6. Number of leaders in the village : Public leader / village leader/ teacher/businessman/government official/students : boys and girls

D. Development : Pre and Post Independence Period

1. *Agriculture / Economy :*
   (a) Number of crops practised in a year.
   (b) Introduction of non-agricultural tools/irrigation system.
   (c) Acceptance of Government supplied seeds and fertilizers.
   (d) Annual income.
   (e) Sources of income : Agriculture/business/service.

2. *Communication*

   (a) Number of roads connected with the village.
   (b) Introduction of railway line and its benefits.

(c) Other agents of communication of the people.

^. *Health & Education*

(a) General health of the people.
(b) Faith in black magic and medicine and treatment of disease.
(c) Attitude towards medical treatment.
(d) Hospital/Dispensary/Family Planning Centre confined to the village.
(e) Drinking water facilities : Tube well/well/pond.
(f) Percentage of literacy.
(g) Number of students - boys/girls in L.P./M.E./H.E./College/University.
(h) School/Library/Co-operatives/Association.
(i) Attitude of the people towards development.

E. Remarks

(b) *INTERVIEW SCHEDULE* *(SCHEDULE IV)*

Sl. No. Confidential.

Acculturation, Communication and Development among the Mishings (Miris) in Assam.

Investigator	*Supervisor*
Jatin Mipun. M.A.	Dr. S.M. Dubey, M.A., Ph. D.
Research Scholar	Professor and Head.
Deptt. of Sociology	Deptt. of Sociology
Dibrugarh University (Assam)	Dibrugarh University (Assam)

A. Personal Background

1. Name :
2. Present occupation :
3. Place of birth :

4. Age : (approximate years)
5. Sex : Male/Female
6. Marital Status : Married/Unmarried/ Widow/Divorced/ Widowers
7. Religion :
8. Clan :
9. Educational Qualification : Illiterate/Primary/Under-matric/Matriculate/Graduate Post-Graduate/Professional Degree (B.E.) (M.B.B.S.) or any other
10. Annual Income of the family from all sources (approximate in Rupees) : Rs.

B. Family Background

1. Nature of Family Joint/Nuclear
2. Total Members of the Family :
3. Relationship with the members in the Family :

Sl. No.	Name	Age	Sex	Marital Status	Education	Occupation	Incor	Relationship
1.								
2.								
3.								
4.								
5.								
6.								

C. Acculturation

Religion

1. Do you visit *Namghar*? : Yes/No

2. If yes, please mention the frequency	:	Regularly/ Frequently/ Occasionally
3. Do you visit *Satras*?	:	Yes/No.
4. If yes, please mention the frequency	:	Regularly/ Frequently/ Occasionally
5. What are the Hindu Gods and Goddesses worshipped by you?	(a) (c)	(b) (d)
6. Do you participate in the *pujas*?	:	
(a) Durga	:	Yes/No
(b) Saraswati	:	Yes/No
(c) Sakti	:	Yes/No
7. If yes, why? (Write down the serial number where applicable)	:	Only for enjoyment/I believe in those *pujas*/ Cannot say
8. Whether these *pujas* are performed by your family or not?	:	Yes/No

Food Habits.

1. Do you take		
(a) Tea	:	Yes/No
(b) Milk	:	Yes/No
(c) Pork	:	Yes/No
(d) Rice Beer	:	Yes/No
2. If yes, how?(write down the serial number where applicable	:	Regularly/ Frequently/ Occasionally
3. Do you take rice in the Hotel?	:	Yes/No
4. If not, why?	:	Due to maintenance of purity/Due to lack of money/any other
5. Do you think that Apong is being replaced by tea and others in your family	:	Yes/No

Language

1. What languages you can speak/read/write and understand?

Sl. No.	Language	Speak	Read	Write	Understand
(a) Assamese					
(b) Bengali					
(c) Hindi					
(d) English					
(e) Any Other					

2. What are the sources of knowing languages? (write down the serial of the above where applicable) : Students/Leaders/ Medium of instruction/ Marketing centres/ Traders/any others

House

1. Type of House
   (a) Assam type pucca house
   (b) R.C.C. Building
   (c) House of wooden platform
   (d) Traditional Chung Ghar

2. If constructed a new house, when the house was constructed? :
3. What are reasons of its construction? (in order of reference)
   1. Education
   2. Sound economic condition
   3. Influence of non-Tribal Assamese
   4. Any other

4. Do you have the plan to construct new type of house in future? : Yes/No

Dress and House Hold Utensils:

1. Whether traditional dress is being used or not in your family?

Family member	Being used	Not being used
Male		
Female		
Children		

2. Whether weaving is still done or not in your family? : Yes/No
3. If yes, is it sufficient to meet the requirement? : Yes/No
4. What is your opinion towards : Like/Dislike/ Neutral
5. Whether modern dress is being used or not? :

Family members	Being used	Not being used
Male		
Female		
Children		

6. Who first introduced modern dress in your family? : Grandfather/ Father/yourself/ your children/ any other
7. Which are responsible for the changing dress pattern in your family (in order of preference)? : Education/Sound economic condition/ unpopularity of weaving/ neighbouring

non-Tribal
Assamese/any
other

8. What are household utensils you have possessed? :

Sl. No.	Traditional Utensils	Modern Utensils
1.		
2.		
3.		
4.		
5.		
6.		

D. Communication

1. Are you possessing
   - (a) Radio Yes/No
   - (b) Bicycle Yes/No
   - (c) Transistor Yes/No
   - (d) Car Yes/No
2. Are you contributing newspaper : Yes/No
3. If yes, please mention the following :

Sl. No.	Paper	Language				
		Assamese	Bengali	Hindi	English	Any other
1.						
2.						
3.						
4.						

4. Do you travel by
   - (a) Bus : Yes/No
   - (b) Train : Yes/No
   - (c) Ferry : Yes/No
5. If yes, for which purpose usually travel? (in order of preference, write down the serial number where applicable) :
   1. For service
   2. For marketing
   3. To visit other place
   4. Only for

enjoyment
5. Any other purpose

E. Development

Economy

1. What is your present occupation? : Cultivation/Business/ Govt. service/any other

2. Please state the particulars of occupation of your three Generation :

Sl. No.	Generation	Main occupation	Subsidiary occupation
1.	Grandfather		
2.	Father		
3.	Self		

3. If your occupation is cultivation do you practise improved methods? : Yes/No

4. If yes, which are : Chemical fertilizer/Insecticide/ Irrigation/Any other.

5. Whether your production is sufficient for your family? : Yes/No

6. If, not, what alternatives are taken to maintain your family? : Part time labour/ Business/Service/ Depended on Cottage Industry/ Any other

7. Do you sell the following items:

Item		
(1) Agricultural production	:	Yes/No
(2) Production of Cottage Industry	:	Yes/No
(3) Domestic Animal	:	Yes/No
(4) Any other	:	Yes/No

8. If yes, where do you invest the income? (in order of preference) : 1. In cultivation for more production
2. Only for consumptior
3. For the education of the children.
4.Only for enjoyment
5.Any other

9. Have you heard about 20 point economic programme : Yes/No

10. If yes, what benefits you are deriving out of it? (a) (b) (c) (d)

Health and Education :

1. What is your opinion towards medical treatment? Like/Dislike/Neutral

2. Do you support family scheme? : Yes/No

3. If not, why? Do not know/do not get facilities/feel shy/do not like/ any other

4. Please note down the birth and death rates of last thirty years of your family :

Sl. No.	Year	Birth (in number)	Death (in number)
1.	1940-1950		
2.	1950-1960		
3.	1960-1970		

5. Kindly mention educational attainments of the following generation of your family :

Sl. No.	Generation	Educational attainment	Training if any
1.	Grandfather		
2.	Father		
3.	Self		

6. Do you send your children to the school?	:	Yes/No
7. If not, why?	:	Unsound economic condition/As they are engaged in cultivation/ Any other
8. What type of education you are going to offer to your children?	:	General/Law/Professional (B.E., M.B.B.S., etc.)/ Any other
9. According to you which are the essential requirements of developments of your community? (in order of preference)		1. Much acculturation is necessary 2. Improved communication system 3. More agricultural production 4. Proper marketing centre 5. Proper education 6. Leaving of social evils 7. Proper leadership 8. Any other

APPENDIX III

GLOSSARY

Donyee-Po:lo	:	(the Sun and the Moon): The Mishings regard *Donyee-po:lo* as their ancestors. They regard the Moon as their father and the Sun as their mother. In any ritual performance, they first recite the name of *Ane Donyee* (Mother Sun) and *Abu Po:lo* (Father Moon).
The Murong	:	Dormitory of the Mishings. It is gradually extinguishing among them.
The Kebang	:	Village Council. It is still active in giving judgements in disputes. There are *Kebang* in State and district levels, viz. All Assam Mishing Ban Kebang and the Bane Kebangs in the district of Assam.
Namghar	:	The religious institution of the Mishings. It is also the religious institution of the non-tribal Assamese population of Assam.
Satras	:	The monasteries, mostly situated in Majuli Subdivision of Sibsagar district.
Kewalia or Kalhanghati or Nisamalia	:	The religion of the Mishings. It is the product of animism and Hinduism.
Miboo or Miri	:	The indigenous village priest of the Mishings.
Sadhu Bura or Bhakat	:	The Head of all religious activities of the Mishings. Bhakats are of two types, viz. *Poka Bhakat* (ripe disciple) and *Kencha Bhakat* (raw or non-converted). The position of *Kencha Bhakat* is next to *Poka Bhakat* in Mishing Society.
Ali-ai-Ligang, Po:rag	:	The famous festivals of the Mishings. Ali-ai Ligang or the Spring dance festival is celebrated on Wednesday of the month of *Falgun* of Indian Calendar. The main aim of the festival is to pray Mother Earth for production *Ahu* paddy. Po:rag is also connected with agriculture. The festival marks the harvesting time of paddy.

Oi-nitom	:	The most famous folk song of the Mishings. They express their innermost feelings through *Oi-nitom.* It has played part and parcel of any type of dance and merry-making
Apong	:	The home-made rice beer of the Mishings. It is of two types, viz. *Nagin Apong* and *Po:ro Apong*. It is their most popular drink.

1. Approach towards Mishing villages, Ferry and boats still play major role of communication and transportation among the Mishing villagers.

2. Mishing village with modern facility like electricity.

3. Mishing dwelling house known as *Ukum* or *Chung ghor*, house on piles above the ground with T.V. antenna which indicates possession of T.V. for widening their knowledge.

The *Mu:rong*, the dormitory essential for performance of Puja and festival like *PO:rag* and *Ali-ai-ligang*. The *Mu:rong* is no longer a permanent structure visible in Mishing villages. Temporary construction is done only when situation demands.

5. An old Mishing couple.

The *Miboo*, the traditional priest of the Mishings. The *Miboo* is on the verse of extinction because of new-Vaishavite movement in Assam and the influence of Hinduism among the Mishings.

7. Mishing lady busy in weaving on her loom, Except the design on the woven clothes, the loom is similar to that of non-tribal Assamese.

8. The product of traditional Mishing dresses from loom.

9. The *gadu* or *Miri-jim*, prestigious product of Mishing loom, usually otters as a gift by a mother to her newly married son.

10. Gam-Yamnam, welcome to the leader in Mishing festivals. The dhoti and pagri are similar to that of the non-tribal Assamese.

11. Offering prayer to Mother-earth for good production of *Ahu* paddy in *Ali-ai-ligang*, spring dance festival of the Mishings.

12. Sacrificing pig in Dodgang, puja for the ancestors or ancestor-worship.

13. Mishing women husking paddy for rice in traditional *Ki : par.*

14. Mishing women preparing rice beer known as *Po : ro Apong* and *nogin apong*, essential for any pujas and festivals of the Mishings.

15. Mishing dance. The dresses of the dancing girls are product of Mishing loom, but the style of wearing is of non-tribal Assamese.

Index

Acculturation, 145
African Gods & the catholic saints, 3
Age group & marital status of the respondents, 44
Agricultural innovation & self-sufficiency, 103
Ahom-chutia conflict, 64
Alternatives to maintain the family of Respondents, 104
Amaya Bhakati, 56
Analysis of preceding chapters, 42
Asian drama, 1968, 6
Assamese peasantry, 97

Bahir, 34
Bhagavat Gita, 65
Bhagavatia, 56
Bhugali bihu, 125
Bighas, 33
Books/articles in Assamese for reference, 139
Brahmaputra valley, 15
Burman, Roy, 78

Case studies, 39
Caste-tribe relationship, 124
Changing dress pattern, 71
Chemical fertilizers, 103
Chung Ghar, 68
Chutia Kingdom (1376 AD-1500 AD), 18
Chutia-Miri, 21
Clan and Kinship Organisation, 20
Classification, tabulation & editing, 40
Construction of modern type houses, 67-68
Communication by, 153
Communication network of the mishings, 88

Daily labour, 104
Deka Bora (messenger of boys), 80
Demographic composition, 36
Dhoti, 73
Dibrugarh, 18
Differential levels of development, 118
District-wise population of Scheduled Tribes, 17
Dobur puja, 81
Doley clan, 20
Doley, Ganesh, 46
Doley, Jobalung, 34
Doley, Kanai, 58

Doley, Kanta, 92
Doley, Manuram, 106
Domestic weaving & attitude towards mill-made clothes, 70
Donyee-Polo, 98
Dress & house hold utensils, 152
Dress of the Mishings, 68
Dress pattern of men & women, 146
Duhutimukh village, location of, 33
Dumer (towel), 69

Economy, 154
Education of frequency of visiting Namghar, 59
Education of the Villagers, 109-11
Education Qualification & use of mass media, 90
Establishment of Rapport, 40

Falgun, month of, 27
Family background, 149
Family planning & attitude towards Medical Sciences, 110
Festivals, 26
Field experience, 40
Folk songs and folk dances, 28
Food habit, 60-62, 146

General articles for references, 129-39
General description of village, 145
Gandharba Vivaha, 25,44
Ghurye, G.S., 121
Guput dharma, 56

Health & Education, 148
Hindu hierarchy, 124
Hindu Society, 78
History background of three villages, 34
Household Schedule, 38
House, 146

Identification of variables, 41
Impact of Hinduism, 122
Impact of the marketing centres, 87-89
Indo-Mongoloid tribe, 1
Indo-Tibeto-Burman languages, 62
Interview Schedule, 39
Interaction & communication with religious political & educational elites, 91
Introduction of Railways & its impact, 85-87
Introduction of roads & its impact on the mishings, 81-85
Investigator & Supervisor, 148

Jajmani, 124
Jhoom cultivation, 103
Journals for reference, 140-44

Kaccha mati ghar, 123
Kardong, Sambhuram, 100
Kali bihu, 125
Kebang (village council), 80
Kewal dharma, 56
Kewalia, 56
Koch of the Garo hills, 78
Kumbang, Brikuram, 34

Lakhimpur, 32

Language, 146
Levels of communication in Mohmora, Duhutimukh & Barpamua Villages, 93-94
Levels of development among mishings, 99
L.P. School in Mohmora, 37
Machine-made tools, 147

Maiki Bora (messenger of the girls), 80
Mantras, 65
Marriage, 22
Miboo (priest), 26
Mishings language, 62
Mishing Society, 73
Mohmora (place of death of buffalows), 34
Moon (*Polo*), 19
Mother-Earth, 27

Namghar (place of worship), 56
Narah, Moheswar, 46
North-East India, 78-79

Occupation of the Respondents, 101

Padun, Moni, 106
Pak Ghar, 68
Pattern of houses, 65
Paw, Maghar, 100
Pegu clan, 20
Pegu, Debeswar, 53
Personal background, 148
Physical mobility, 97
Population of Mohmora, Duhutimukh & Barpamua villages, 36
  literacy of, 36-37
Political life, 29
Post & telegraph, Radio listening & newspaper reading, impact of, 89
Pre and post independence period, 147
Preferences given by the Respondents in the investment of their income, 105
Process of acculturation, 54
Puja, 55

Rangali bihu, 125
Ratikhowa dharma, 56
Relationship (man speaking), 23
Religion, 25, 145
Respondents' qualification & causes for sending or not sending children to school, 112
Respondents, 46
  education of, 46
  level of, 47
  annual income of, 47,48-49
  family size & income of, 50-51
  nature & size of family of, 52
Respondents towards development & preference, 114

Socio-cultural change, 117
Sraddha ceremony, 125
Sadhu Bura, 57
Sarah, Mohan, 73
Saro, Mante, 106
Satras, 55
Scheduled tribes population in Assam, 15-16
Shirt (*galuk*), 69
Social life, 20

Sources of knowing different languages by respondents, 63
Subsidiary occupation of three generations of the respondents' family, 102
Sun (*Donyee*), 19

Tools & implements, 72
Traditional notion about health & diseases, 106-9
Tribes of North-East, 54
Type of education preferred by the respondents for their children, 113-16

Vaisnava *Gosains*, 55
Varieties of alternatives, 104
Village Schedule, 37
Visits to Namghar & Satras, 59
Yame-member (Youths), 80